THE
SEAGULL

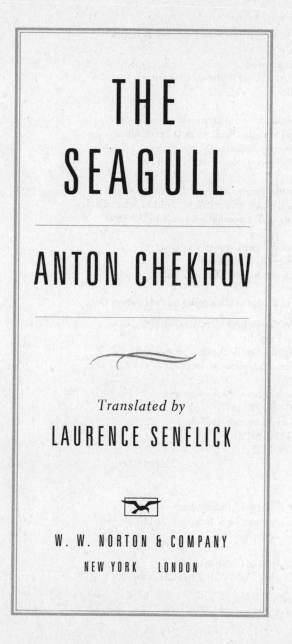

THE SEAGULL

ANTON CHEKHOV

Translated by
LAURENCE SENELICK

W. W. NORTON & COMPANY

NEW YORK   LONDON

For information about permission to reproduce
selections from this book, write to Permissions,
W. W. Norton & Company, Inc.,
.500 Fifth Avenue, New York, NY 10110

For information about special discounts for bulk
purchases, please contact W. W. Norton Special Sales
at specialsales@wwnorton.com or 800-233-4830

Manufacturing by Courier Westford
Book design by JAM Design
Production manager: Devon Zahn

Library of Congress Cataloging-in-Publication Data

Chekhov, Anton Pavlovich, 1860–1904.
[Chaika. English]
The seagull / Anton Chekhov ; translated
by Laurence Senelick. — 1st ed.
p. cm.
Includes bibliographical references.
ISBN 978-0-393-33817-1 (pbk.)
I. Senelick, Laurence. II. Title.
PG3456.C5S46 2010
891.72'3 — dc22

2010018095

W. W. Norton & Company, Inc.
500 Fifth Avenue, New York, N.Y. 10110
www.wwnorton.com

W. W. Norton & Company Ltd.
Castle House, 75/76 Wells Street, London W1T 3QT

1 2 3 4 5 6 7 8 9 0

This edition is dedicated to the cast and
crew of the Balch Arena Theater
production at Tufts University.

CONTENTS

THE
SEAGULL

ANTON CHEKHOV'S BRIEF LIFE

Anton Pavlovich Chekhov was born in the town of Taganrog on the sea of Azov in southern Russia on January 17, 1860,[1] the third of six children, five boys and a girl. He might have been born a serf, as his father, Pavel Yegorovich, had, for the Emancipation came only in 1861; but his grandfather, a capable and energetic estate manager named Yegor Chekh, had prospered so well that in 1841 he had purchased his freedom along with his family's. Anton's mother, Yevgeniya Morozova, was the orphaned daughter of a cloth merchant and a subservient spouse to her despotic husband. To their children, she imparted a sensibility he lacked: Chekhov would later say, somewhat unfairly, that they inherited their talent from their father and their soul from their mother.[2]

The talent was displayed in church. Beyond running a small grocery store where his sons served long hours—"In my childhood, there was no childhood," Anton was later to report[3]—Pavel Chekhov had a taste for the outward trappings of religion. This was satisfied by unfailing observance of the rites of the Eastern Orthodox Church, daily family worship, and, especially, liturgical music. He enrolled his sons in a choir that he founded and conducted, and he aspired to be a pillar of the community.

Taganrog, its once-prosperous port now silted up and neglected, had a population that exceeded fifty thousand during Chekhov's boyhood. Its residents included wealthy Greek families, the shipbuilding interests, and a large number of Jews, Tatars, and Armenians. The town benefited from such public amenities of the tsarist civil administration as a pretentious-looking *gymnasium*, which the Chekhov boys attended, for one of Pavel's aims was to procure his children the level of education needed for entry into the professions. The upward mobility of the Chekhov generations is reflected in the character of Lopakhin in *The Cherry Orchard*, a self-made millionaire whose ancestors had been serfs on the estate he succeeds in purchasing. Chekhov's father, born a serf, had risen from *meshchanin*, or petty bourgeois,[4] to be the member of a merchant guild; and Chekhov himself, as a physician and writer, became influential on the national scene. He was a model of the *raznochinets*, or person of no settled rank, who began to dominate Russian society in the latter half of the nineteenth century.

To impede mass advancement, the tsarist curriculum laid great stress on Greek and Latin. One recalls the schoolmaster Kulygin in *Three Sisters* chuckling over the fate of a classmate who missed promotion because he could not master the *ut consecutivum* construction. Schoolmasters are usually portrayed by Chekhov as narrow-minded, obsequious, and unimaginative, no doubt the result of his own observations as he studied the classics, German, Russian, and, for a brief time, French. His best subject was Scripture. School days were lightened by the fairy tales of his nanny, the picaresque reminiscences of his mother, vacations spent on the estate his grandfather managed, fishing, swimming, and, later, visits to the theater.

As a boy, Chekhov was stage-struck. Although it was against school regulations, he and his classmates, often in false whiskers and dark glasses, frequented the gallery of the active and imposing Taganrog Playhouse. He was also the star performer in domestic theatricals, playing comic roles such as the Mayor in *The Inspector* and the scrivener Chuprun in the Ukrainian folk opera *The Military Magician*. While still at school, he wrote a drama called *Without Patrimony* and a vaudeville (a farce with songs) called *The Hen Has Good Reason to Cluck*. Later, while a medical student, he tried to revise them, even as he completed another farce, *The Cleanshaven Secretary with the Pistol*, which his younger brother Mikhail recalls as being very funny. Never submitted to the government censorship office, which passed plays or forbade them from performance, it is now lost.

By 1876 Pavel Chekhov had so mismanaged his business that, fearing imprisonment for debt, he stole off to the next town, where he took the train to Moscow. There his two elder sons, Aleksandr and Nikolay, were pursuing their studies. He had already stopped paying his dues to the merchant guild and had reverted to the status of *meshchanin*. Whether Anton suffered a psychic trauma at this loss of caste, as had the young Henrik Ibsen when *his* father went bankrupt, is matter for speculation. Certainly, the repercussions felt at the sale of the home left their trace on many of his plays, including *Platonov* and *The Cherry Orchard*. Dispos-

sessed of home and furniture, his mother and the three young-
est children also departed for Moscow, abandoning Anton in a
house now owned by a friend of his father's. He had to support
himself by tutoring during the three years before he graduated.
He did not rejoin his family until Easter 1877, his fare paid by his
university-student brother Aleksandr. This first visit to Moscow
and its theaters set standards by which he henceforth judged the
quality of life in the provinces. Suddenly, Taganrog began to look
provincial.

Just before Anton Chekhov left Taganrog for good, a public
library opened. This enabled him to read classics such as *Don
Quixote* and *Hamlet*, a work he was to cite recurrently, and, like
any Victorian schoolboy, *Uncle Tom's Cabin* and the adventure
stories of Thomas Mayne Reid. Heavier reading included philo-
sophic works that enjoyed a high reputation at the time, such as
Thomas Henry Buckle's positivist and skeptical survey of Euro-
pean culture, *The History of Civilization in England*. Later in life,
Chekhov took a wry view of this omnivorous autodidacticism, and
had the clumsy bookkeeper Yepikhodov in *The Cherry Orchard*
allude to Buckle's works as a token of self-improvement.

It was at this time that Chekhov began writing prose, sending
comic pieces to Aleksandr in Moscow in the hope that they would
be accepted by the numerous comic journals that had sprung up
in the capitals. He made friends with actors, hung around back-
stage, and learned how to make up his face. Two of his school fel-
lows did enter the profession: Aleksandr Vishnevsky, who would
become a charter member of the Moscow Art Theatre, and Nikolay Solovtsov, who was to create the title role in *The Bear*.

In 1879 Chekhov moved to Moscow to enter the medical school at the university, funded by a scholarship from the Taganrog municipal authorities. He arrived to find himself the head of the family, which was still in dire straits and living in a cramped basement flat in a disreputable slum. His father, now a humble clerk in a suburban warehouse, boarded at his office; Aleksandr, a journalist, and Nikolay, a painter, led alcoholic and bohemian lives; his three younger siblings, Ivan, Mariya, and Mikhail, still had to complete their educations. Lodging at home, Chekhov was compelled to carve out a career as a journalist at the same time that he was taking the rigorous five-year course in medicine.

At first, he wrote primarily for humor magazines, contributing anecdotes and extended jokes, sometimes as captions to drawings by Nikolay and others; these brought in a niggardly ten to twelve kopeks a line. Gradually, he diversified into parodies, short stories, and serials, including a murder mystery, *The Shooting Party*, and a romance that proved so popular it was filmed several times in the days of silent cinema (*Futile Victory*). He was a reporter at the trial of the CEOs of a failed bank. He became a close friend of Nikolay Leykin, editor of the periodical *Splinters of Petersburg Life*, to which he was a regular contributor from 1883. He conducted a theatrical gossip column, which won him entry to all the greenrooms and side-scenes in Moscow. And he partook of his brothers' bohemianism. He wrote to an old school chum in a letter his Soviet editors provided only in expurgated form: "I was on a spree all last night and, 'cept for a 3-ruble drunk didn't . . . or catch . . . I'm just about to go on a spree again."[5] His writing at this time was published under a variety of pseudonyms, the best known being Antosha Chekhonte, from a schoolboy nickname. He also found time to revise *Without Patrimony*, which he seriously hoped would be staged; turned down by the leading actress to whom he submitted it, it was burnt by its author. Chekhov always took failure in the theater hard. However, two variant copies survived, minus the title page. It was first published in 1923. It has since become known as *Platonov*, after the central character.

The year 1884 was critical in Chekhov's life. At the age of twenty-four, he set up as a general practitioner and, influenced by reading the English social critic Herbert Spencer, began research on a history of medicine in Russia. That December he had bouts of spitting blood, which his medical expertise might have led him to diagnose as a symptom of pulmonary tuberculosis. No outside observer would have suspected this active, well-built, handsome young man was suffering from a mortal illness. Only in his last years did he become a semi-invalid, and, until that time, he kept up the pretence that his symptoms were not fatal. This subterfuge was not carried on simply to allay his family's anxieties. He wilfully strove to ignore the forecast of his own mortality and regularly discounted the gravity of his condition.

Eighteen eighty-four also saw the publication of his first collection of stories, pointedly entitled *Fairy Tales of Melpomene*: the muse of tragedy compressed into pithy anecdotes of the life of actors. Chekhov had found more prestigious and better-paying periodicals to take his stories and was now an expert on Moscow life.

He had an opportunity to amplify his subject matter when he and his family began to spend summers in the country, first with his brother Ivan, master of a village school, and then in a cottage on the estate of the Kiselyov family. It was during those summers that Chekhov gained first-hand knowledge of the manor house setting he employed in many of his plays, and made the acquaintance of the officers of a battery, who turn up as characters in *Three Sisters*. Chekhov's artistic horizons also expanded, for the Kiselyovs, intimates of the composer Chaikovsky, were devoted to classical music. Another summer visitor to become a lifelong friend was the painter Isaak Levitan, whose impressionistic landscapes are graphic counterparts of Chekhov's descriptions.

The following year Chekhov's literary career took a conspicuous upward turn. On a visit to St. Petersburg, Chekhov had been embarrassed by the acclaim that greeted him, because he recognized that much of his output had been hasty and unrevised. "If I had known that that was how they were reading me," he wrote his brother Aleksandr, on January 4, 1886, "I would not have written like a hack." Such stories as "Grief" and "The Huntsman," both from 1885, had already displayed a new care in technique and seriousness in subject matter. Shortly thereafter, he received a letter from Dmitry Grigorovich, the *doyen* of Russian critics, singling him out as the most promising writer of his time and urging him to take his talent more seriously. Although Antosha Chekhonte continued to appear in print for a few more years, Anton Chekhov made his first bow in the powerful Petersburg newspaper *New Times*. Its editor, Aleksey Suvorin, had risen from peasant origins to become a tycoon and a leading influence-monger in the conservative political camp. He and Chekhov were to be closely allied, although their friendship would later founder when Suvorin promoted the anti-Semitic line during the Dreyfus affair.

During the years when he was winning recognition as a writer of short stories, Chekhov made two further attempts to write for the theater. With the first, *Along the Highway* (1885), he came up against the obstacle of the censor, who banned it on the grounds that it was a "gloomy, squalid play." The other piece, the monologue *The Evils of Tobacco*, was, like many of his early "dramatic études," written with a specific actor in mind. It first appeared in 1886 in a St. Petersburg newspaper, and Chekhov kept revising it, publishing the final version, virtually a new work, in his collected writings of 1903. Farces he sketched out with collaborators never got beyond the planning stage.

Between 1886 and 1887, Chekhov published one hundred and sixty-six titles while practicing medicine. Such fecundity boosted his fame but wore him out. His health and his temper both began to fray. Profiting from an advance from Suvorin, Chekhov returned to southern Russia in 1887, a trip that produced remarkable work. The stories that ensued signaled his emergence as a leading writer of serious fiction. The novella "The Steppe" (1888) was published in *The Northern Herald*, one of the so-called fat, or weighty, journals that had introduced the writing of Ivan Turgenev and Lev Tolstoy and served as organs of public opinion. That same year, Chekhov was awarded the Pushkin Prize for Literature by the Imperial Academy of Science for his collection *In the Gloaming*. One of the most enthusiastic instigators of this honor had been the writer Vladimir Nemirovich-Danchenko, who would later play an important role in establishing Chekhov's reputation as a dramatist.

The Northern Herald was liberal in its politics, its editor, Aleksey Pleshcheev, a former prisoner in Siberia with Dostoevsky. Typically, Chekhov was able to be friendly with Pleshcheev and Suvorin at the same time, and he continued to contribute to *New Times*. His reluctance to be identified with any one faction exposed him to much acrimonious criticism from members of both camps, and especially from the progressive left. The writer Katherine Mansfield pointed out that the "problem" in literature is an invention of the nineteenth century. One of the legacies of Russian "civic criticism" of the 1840s was the notion that a writer had an obligation to engage with social problems and offer solutions, making his works an uplifting instrument of enlightenment. This usually meant espousing a doctrinaire political platform. Chekhov, perhaps fortified by his medical training, treasured his objectivity and steadfastly refrained from taking sides, even when his sympathies were easy to ascertain. "God keep us from generalizations," he wrote. "There are a great many opinions in this world and a good half of them are professed by people who have never had any problems."

Between 1886 and 1890, his letters discuss his objectivity and his "monthly change" of opinions, which readers preferred to see as the views of his leading characters. To his brother Aleksandr he insisted on May 10, 1886, that in writing no undue emphasis be placed on political, social, or economic questions. In another letter to Suvorin, on October 27, 1888, Chekhov wrote that the author must be an observer, posing questions but not supplying the answers. It is the reader who brings subjectivity to bear. Not that an author should be aloof, but his own involvement in a problem should be invisible to the reader, he explained to Suvorin, on April 1, 1890:

> You reproach me for my objectivity, calling it indifference to good and evil, absence of ideals and ideas, etc. You want me to say, when I depict horse thieves: horse-stealing is a bad thing. But that's been known for a long time now, without my help, hasn't it? Let juries pass verdicts on horse thieves; as for me, my work is only to show them as they are.

The year before "The Steppe" appeared, Chekhov had at last had a play produced; the manager Fyodor Korsh had commissioned *Ivanov* and staged it at his Moscow theater on November 19, 1887. It was a decided if controversial success. As Chekhov wrote to Aleksandr, "Theater buffs say they've never seen so much ferment, so much unanimous applause *cum* hissing, and never ever heard so many arguments as they saw and heard at my play" (November 20, 1887). It was taken up by the Alexandra Theatre, the Imperial dramatic playhouse in St. Petersburg, and produced there on January 31, 1889, after much hectic rewriting in an attempt to make the playwright's intentions clearer and to take into account the strengths and weaknesses of the new cast.

The theme of a protagonist fettered by a sick wife and want

of money was a distorted reflection of Chekhov's own situation. His family obligations kept his nose to the grindstone, and he felt guilty whenever he traveled away. Yet the success of *Ivanov* and the curtain-raisers *The Bear* and *The Proposal* (1888–1889) had put Chekhov at a premium as a dramatist. Urged on by Korsh and others, and unable to make headway on a full-length novel, Chekhov hoped to collaborate with Suvorin on a new comedy; when the publisher begged off, Chekhov completed it himself as *The Wood Goblin* (1889). It was promptly turned down by the state-subsidized theaters of Petersburg and Moscow, which regarded it as more a dramatized story than an actable play. They recommended that Chekhov give up writing for the stage. A production at a private theater in Moscow was received with apathy bordering on contempt, and may have helped provide the impetus for a decision Chekhov would soon make to go to Sakhalin, ten thousand miles away. Throughout 1888 and 1889, Chekhov also tended to his brother Nikolay, who was dying of tuberculosis; after Nikolay's death, Chekhov experienced both guilt and a foreboding of his own mortality, which brought on the mood conveyed in "A Dismal Story" (1889), in which a professor of medicine contemplates his frustrated ideals and imminent demise. The author's mood was at its lowest ebb.

Secure in his reputation and income at the age of thirty, Chekhov sought to cast off this despondency by traveling to Sakhalin, the Russian Devil's Island, in 1890; the eighty-one-day journey was arduous, for the Trans-Siberian railway had not yet been built. The enterprise may have been inspired by a Tolstoyan wish to practice altruism or it may have been an ambitious project to write a magnum opus of "medical geography." In any case, the ensuing documentary study of the penal colony was a model of socially engaged field research, and may have led to prison reforms. On a more personal level, it intensified a new strain of pessimism in Chekhov's work, for, despite his disclaimers, he began to be bothered by his lack of outlook or mission.

No sooner had Chekhov returned, via Hong Kong, Singapore, and Ceylon, than he made his first excursion to Western Europe, accompanying Suvorin. His initial enthusiasm for Vienna, Venice, and Naples began to wane by the time he visited Nice, Monte Carlo, and Paris, and he was eager to get back to work. In Russia, with the writing routines resumed, the sense of enslavement returned. This mood was modulated by a flirtation with a family friend, Lidiya (Lika) Mizinova, who invested more significance in the relationship than he did. Her subsequent affair and illegitimate child with the married writer Ignaty Potapenko would be exploited by Chekhov in *The Seagull* (although he hoped his own circle would not spot the similarities).

The steady flow of royalties enabled Chekhov in 1891 to buy a farmstead at Melikhovo, some fifty miles south of Moscow, where he settled his parents and siblings. There he set about "to squeeze the last drop of slave out of his system" (as he wrote to Suvorin on January 7, 1889); "a modern Cincinnatus," he planted a cherry orchard, installed a flush toilet, and became a lavish host. This rustication had a beneficial effect on both his literary work and his humanitarianism. He threw himself into schemes for building roads and schools and opened a clinic to provide free medical treatment, improving peasants' minds and bodies. During the cholera epidemic of 1892–1893, he served as an overworked member of the sanitary commission and head of the famine relief board. These experiences found their way into the activities of Dr. Astrov in *Uncle Vanya*.

During this period, Chekhov composed masterful stories that explored the dead ends of life: "The Duel" (1891), "Ward No. 6" (1892), "The Black Monk," "A Woman's Kingdom," "The Student" (all 1894), "Three Years" (1895), "The House with the Mansard," "My Life" (both 1896), and "Peasants" (1897), carefully wrought prose pieces of great psychological subtlety. They recurrently dwell on the illusions indispensable to making life bearable, the often frustrated attempts at contact with one's fellow man, the inexorable pull of inertia preventing people from realizing their potential for honesty and happiness. Chekhov's attitude is clinically critical, but always with a keen eye for the sympathetic details that lead the reader to a deeper understanding.

For several years, Chekhov abandoned the theater, except for some monologues and one-act farces. Not until January 1894 did he announce that he had again begun a play, only to deny it a year later, in a letter to V. V. Bilibin: "I am not writing a play and, altogether, I have no inclination to write any. I am grown old, and I have lost my burning ardor. I should like to write a novel 100 miles long" (January 18, 1895). Nine months after that he was to break the news to Suvorin, "Can you imagine, I am writing a play which I shall probably not finish before the end of November. I am writing it not without pleasure, though I swear horribly at the conventions of the stage. A comedy, three women's parts, six men's, four acts, a landscape (view of a lake); a great deal of conversation about literature, little action, five tons of love" (October 21, 1895).

The comedy was *The Seagull*, which had a rocky opening night at St. Petersburg's Alexandra Theatre in 1896: the actors misunderstood it, the audience misapprehended it. Despite protestations of unconcern to Suvorin ("I dosed myself with castor oil, took a cold bath—and now I would not even mind writing another play"; October 22, 1896), Chekhov fled to Melikhovo, where he renounced playwriting. Although *The Seagull* grew in public favor in subsequent performances, Chekhov disliked submitting his work to the judgment of literary cliques and claques. Yet barely one year after the event, a new drama from his hand appeared in the 1897 collection of his plays: *Uncle Vanya*, a reworking of the earlier *The Wood Goblin*. It was widely performed in provincial capitals, where the residents found it reflected their dreary lives.

It was during this year that Chekhov's illness was definitively diagnosed as tuberculosis, and he was compelled to leave Melikhovo for a milder climate. For the rest of his life, he shuttled between Yalta on the Black Sea and various French and German spas, with occasional business trips to Moscow. He had a house constructed in the Yalta suburb of Autka. To pay for it, and to cover the new expenses his multiple residences created, Chekhov sold all he had written before 1899, excepting the plays, to the publisher Marks for the flat fee of 75,000 rubles (in current purchasing power, approximately $81,000), along with the reprint rights to any future stories. It was an improvident move. Marks had had no idea of the size of Chekhov's output and had underpaid. The error in calculation may have induced Chekhov to return to playwriting as a more lucrative activity.

The remainder of his dramatic career was bound up with the fortunes of the Moscow Art Theatre, founded in 1897 by his friend Nemirovich-Danchenko and the wealthy dilettante K. S. Alekseev, who acted under the name Konstantin Stanislavsky. Chekhov was one of the original shareholders in the enterprise. He admired his friends' announced program of ensemble playing, their serious attitude to art, and a repertory of high literary quality. At the opening production, Aleksey Tolstoy's blank-verse historical drama *Tsar Feodor Ioannovich*, his eye was caught by Olga Knipper, the young actress who played the tsarina. With only slight misgivings Chekhov allowed the Art Theatre to revive *The Seagull* at the close of its first season. Stanislavsky, as co-director, had greater misgivings; he did not understand the play. But a heavily atmospheric production won over the audience, and the play was a resounding success. The Moscow Art Theatre adopted an art-nouveau seagull as its insignia and henceforth regarded Chekhov as its house dramatist. When the Imperial Maly Theatre insisted on revisions to *Uncle Vanya*, which had been playing throughout the provinces for years, Chekhov withdrew the play from them and allowed the Art Theatre to stage its Moscow premiere. *Three Sisters* (1901) was written with Art Theatre actors in mind.

Chekhov's chronic reaction to the production of his plays was revulsion, and so two months after the opening of *Three Sisters*, he was declaring, to Olga Knipper, "I will never write for the theater again. One can write for the theater in Germany, in Sweden, even in Spain, but not in Russia, where dramatists get no respect, are kicked by hooves and forgiven neither success nor failure" (March 1, 1901). Nevertheless, he soon was deep into *The Cherry Orchard* (1904), tailoring the roles to specific Moscow Art players. Each of these productions won Chekhov greater fame as a playwright, even when he himself disagreed with the chosen interpretation of the Art Theatre.

Chekhov languished in Yalta, which he called his "warm Siberia," feeling that he had been shunted to an outpost for the moribund. At the age of forty, in 1900, to the great surprise of his friends and the temporary dismay of his sister Mariya, who had always been his housekeeper, he married the Art Theatre actress Olga Knipper. Chekhov's liaisons with women had been numerous, ranging from a brief engagement in 1886 to Dunya Efros, a Jewish woman who refused to convert to Orthodoxy, to a one-night stand with a Japanese prostitute and a fling with the flamboyant actress Lidiya Yavorskaya. He exercised an involuntary fascination over a certain type of ambitious bluestocking and his fan mail from female admirers was considerable. Some women friends, such as Lidiya Avilova, projected their desires onto an ordinary relationship, casting themselves as Chekhov's Egeria. Whenever the affair became too demanding or the woman too clinging, Chekhov would use irony and playful humor to disengage himself. In his writings, marriage is usually portrayed as a snare and a delusion that mires his characters in spirit-sapping vulgarity. His relationship with Knipper was both high-spirited—she was his "kitten," his "horsie," his "lambkin," his "darling crocodile"—and conveniently remote, for she had to spend much of her time in Moscow, while he convalesced at his villa in Yalta. On those terms, the marriage was a success.

Chekhov's villa, today a museum, became a Mecca for young writers, importunate fans, touring acting companies, and plain freeloaders. Such pilgrimages, though well meant, were not conducive to Chekhov's peace of mind or body, and his health continued to deteriorate. Despite this rapid decline, and the disappointment of a miscarriage Olga suffered in 1902,[6] a deeply lyrical tone suffuses his last writings. His late stories, "The Darling" and "Lady with Lapdog" (both 1899) and "The Bishop" (1902) and "Betrothed" (1903), offer more acceptance of the cyclical nature of life. They also reveal an almost musical attention to the structure and sounds of words, a quality to be remarked as well in the last "comedy," *The Cherry Orchard.*

In December 1903, a failing Chekhov came to Moscow to attend rehearsals of *The Cherry Orchard.* The opening night, January 17, 1904, concided with his name day and the twenty-fifth anniversary of the commencement of his literary activity. Emaciated, hunched over, gravely ill, he did not show up until the second act and sat through the third, after which, to his great bemusement, a ceremony to honor him took place.

In June 1904 the Berlin doctors Chekhov consulted ordered him to Badenweiler, a health resort in the Black Forest. There the forty-four-year-old writer died on July 2. Shortly before his death, the doctor recommended putting an ice pack on his heart. "You don't put ice on an empty heart," Chekhov protested. When they suggested a glass of champagne, his last words came, "It's been a long time since I've drunk champagne." Unconsciously, he echoed the line of the old nurse Marina in *Uncle Vanya*: "It's a long time since I've had noodles."

Chekhov's obsequies were a comedy of errors he might have appreciated. The railway carriage bearing his body to St. Petersburg was stencilled with the label "Fresh Oysters," and, at the Novodevichy cemetery in Moscow, the bystanders spent more time ogling the controversial author Maksim Gorky and the bass singer Fyodor Shalyapin than in mourning the deceased.[7] Finally, and inadvertently, Chekhov's cortège became entangled with that of General Keller, a military hero who had been shipped home from the Far East. Chekhov's friends were startled to hear an army band accompanying the remains of a man who had always been chary of the grand gesture.

NOTES

1 The date given by Chekhov himself, although he would appear to have been born on the 16th. The 17th was his "saint's day" or "name day," the day of St. Anthony after whom he was christened. Dates given here are "Old Style," in accord with the Julian calendar, twelve days behind the Gregorian.

2 M. P. Chekhov, *Vokrug Chekhova* (Moscow: Moskovsky rabochy, 1980), p. 44.

3 Quoted in Ernest Simmons, *Chekhov, A Biography* (Boston: Little, Brown, 1962), p. 6.

4 Peter the Great had established a table of ranks that stratified social status into civil, military, naval, and ecclesiastical hierarchies. In the civil hierarchy, *meshchanin* (literally, townsman) came just above peasant. In *The Seagull*, Treplyov complains that his father had been classified as a *meshchanin* of Kiev, even though he was a famous actor, and the same rank appears on his own passport. He finds it particularly galling since the term had come to imply philistinism.

5 Letter to Dmitry Savelyov, January (?) 1884. All translated quotations from Chekhov's writings and letters are based on *Polnoe sobranie sochineny i pisem*, the complete collected works and letters in thirty volumes published in Moscow in 1974–1983. On the cuts made by Soviet editors, see A. Chudakov, " 'Neprilichnye slova' i oblik klassika. O kupyurakh v izdaniya pisem Chekhova," *Literaturnoe obozrenie* (November 1991): 54–56.

6 Olga's miscarriage is described in a letter of hers to Chekhov (March 31, 1902). However, a controversy has arisen among scholars as to whether it was a miscarriage, an ectopic pregnancy, or something else; moreover, the paternity of the child has been questioned. See the articles of Hugh McLean and Donald Rayfield in *The Bulletin of the North American Chekhov Society* XI, 1 (Summer 2003), and letters in subsequent issues.

7 Maksim Gorky, *Literary Portraits*, trans. Ivy Litvinov (Moscow: Foreign Languages Publishing House, n.d.), pp. 158–159.

CHRONOLOGY OF CHEKHOV'S LIFE

1860. *January 17* (Old Style) / 29 (New Style). Anton Pavlovich Chekhov, third son of the shopkeeper and choirmaster Pavel Yegorovich Chekhov and Yevgeniya Yakovlevna Morozova, is born in Taganrog, a port of the Sea of Azov. He is the grandson of a serf who managed to purchase his liberation.

Aleksandr Ostrovsky's play *Thunderstorm* wins an award from the Academy of Sciences.

1861. Tsar Alexander II abolishes serfdom, but without providing enough land for the emancipated serfs.

1862. Ivan Turgenev's *Fathers and Sons* is published.

Academic freedom restored to Russian universities.

1863. Flogging with birch rods abolished by law.

Konstantin Stanislavsky is born, as Konstantin Alekseev, son of a wealthy textile manufacturer.

Nikolay Chernyshevsky's *What Is to Be Done?*, the gospel of nihilism, is written in prison.

1864. *Zemstvos*, self-governing rural councils, are created.

1865. Lev Tolstoy begins to publish *War and Peace*.

1866. An attempted assassination of the tsar prompts a wave of political reaction, especially in education and the press. Chekhov, as a student, will suffer from the new emphasis on Greek, Latin, and grammar.

Fyodor Dostoevsky's *Crime and Punishment* published.

1867–1879. Chekhov's primary and secondary education in Taganrog in very rigorous schools. He gives lessons, frequents the theater, edits a student newspaper, writes plays now lost.

1868. Dostoevsky's *The Idiot* is published serially.

1871. Dostoevsky's *The Devils* is published.

1872. Special court set up to try treason cases.

1873. Only 227 factories in all of Russia.

Nikolay Nekrasov begins to publish his populist poem *Who Can Be Happy in Russia?*

1874. Trade unions made illegal.

All males over twenty-one, regardless of class, now liable for conscription into the armed forces.

1875. Chekhov writes comic journal *The Stutterer* to amuse his brothers in Moscow.

Tolstoy begins to publish *Anna Karenina*.

1876. Chekhov's father goes bankrupt and moves the family to Moscow, leaving Anton in Taganrog.

1877. Chekhov visits Moscow where he finds his family in penury.

The Russians fight the Turks in the Balkans, ostensibly to free the Christian Slavs from Moslem oppression. An armistice, signed in 1878, greatly reduces the Turkish presence in the Balkans, but the Congress of Berlin humiliates Russia by reducing its spoils to part of Bessarabia.

1878. Chekhov writes plays now lost: *Without Patrimony, He Met His Match,* and *The Hen Has Good Reason to Cluck.*

Public outcries against the government and acts of terrorism increase.

1879. Chekhov finishes high school and in June moves to Moscow, where he enrolls in the medical school of the University of Moscow on a scholarship. Starts to write cartoon captions for the humor magazine *Alarm Clock.*

Dostoevsky begins to publish *The Brothers Karamazov.*

1880. *March.* Chekhov's first short story, "Letter of a Landowner to His Learned Neighbor Dr. Friedrich," is published in the comic journal *The Dragon-fly.*

1880–1887. Chekhov writes for Moscow and St. Petersburg comic journals under pen names including Antosha Chekhonte, Doctor Who's Lost His Patients, Man without a Spleen, and My Brother's Brother.

1881. Chekhov writes play later known as *Platonov* (not published until 1923).

Tsar Alexander II is assassinated; his son, Alexander III, initiates a reign of political repression and social stagnation.

Dostoevsky dies.

1882. *Platonov* is turned down by the Maly Theatre. Chekhov publishes "Late-blooming Flowers."

The imperial monopoly on theater in Moscow and St. Petersburg is abolished. Several private theaters are opened.

Troops are used to suppress student uprisings at the Universities of St. Petersburg and Kazan.

1883. Chekhov publishes "Fat and Lean," "At Sea," and "Christmas Eve."

1884. Chekhov finishes his medical studies and starts general practice in Chikino, outside Moscow. Publishes his first collection of stories, *Fairy Tales of Melpomene,* under the name Antosha Chekhonte. His only attempt at a novel, *The Shooting Party,* serialized in *Daily News.* Writes one-act play, *Along the High Road,* which is censored and not published until 1914.

December. Symptoms of Chekhov's tuberculosis diagnosed.

1885. Chekhov's first trip to St. Petersburg. Meets the publisher Aleksey Suvorin and the painter Isaak Levitan, who become close friends. Romances with Dunya Efros and Nataliya Golden. Publishes "The Huntsman," "Sergeant Prishibeev," and "Grief."

1886.   Chekhov begins writing for Suvorin's conservative newspaper *New Times*. Puts out a second collection of stories, *Motley Tales*, signed both An. P. Chekhov and Antosha Chekhonte.

The eminent Russian critic Dmitry Grigorovich encourages him to pursue his literary career in a more serious fashion. Publishes "The Witch," "The Chorus Girl," "On the Road," and the first version of the comic monologue *The Evils of Tobacco*.

1887.   Chekhov publishes third collection of short stories, *In the Gloaming*, and fourth collection, *Innocent Conversations*, which include "Enemies," "Typhus," "The Siren," and "Kashtanka." Also writes one-act *Swan Song*.

November 19. Ivanov, a full-length play, performed at Korsh's Theatre, Moscow. It receives a mixed press.

1888.   First serious long story, "The Steppe," published in St. Petersburg magazine *Northern Herald*, initiating a new care taken with his writing. One-act farces *The Bear* and *The Proposal* produced to acclaim. *In the Gloaming* wins the Pushkin Prize of the Academy of Sciences.

Student uprisings at the Universities of Moscow, Odessa, Kharkov, and Kazan are put down by the military. The government decrees that all Jews must live within the Pale of Settlement in Eastern Poland and the western provinces of Russia.

Tolstoy publishes his play of peasant life *The Power of Darkness*, but the censor will not allow it to be staged.

Maksim Gorky is arrested for subversion, and is henceforth under police surveillance.

1889. The Social Democratic Working-man's Party is founded.

"A Dismal Story," one of the first of Chekhov's mature stories, published in *Northern Herald*.

January 31. Premiere of the revised *Ivanov* at Alexandra Theatre, St. Petersburg.

October. Chekhov's play *The Wood Goblin* finished. Played at Abramova's Theatre in *December*. The play is poorly received by the critics; he is scolded for "blindly copying everyday life and paying no attention to the requirements of the stage."

1890. According to a letter to Sergey Dyagilev, Chekhov reworks *The Wood Goblin* into *Uncle Vanya*, which will not be published until 1897. Chekhov publishes collection *Glum People*, which includes "Thieves" and "Gusev." Writes one-act comedies, *The Involuntary Tragedian* and *The Wedding*.

April–October. Travels through Siberia to Sakhalin Island, where he visits prison camps and carries out a census. Sails in the Pacific and Indian Oceans.

1891. Six-week trip to Western Europe. Publication of the novella *The Duel* and "Peasant Women." Buys a small farmstead in Melikhovo.

1892. Chekhov settles in Melikhovo with his family.

Work begins on the Trans-Siberian Railway, to be completed in 1905.

Sergey Witte becomes Minister of Finance, and turns Russia into a modern industrial state, increasing industrialism, railways, and Western trade by 1899.

1892–1893.   Severe famines in the grain-growing provinces in the south and along the Volga.

Chekhov acts as head of the district sanitary commission during the cholera epidemic, combats the famine, treats the poorest peasants for free.

Publishes eleven stories, including "My Wife," "The Grasshopper," "Ward No. 6," as well as the one-act farce *The Celebration*.

1893.   Dalliance with Lika Mizinova, whom he decides not to marry, but who sees herself as a prototype for Nina in *The Seagull*. *The Island of Sakhalin* published serially. Publishes "An Anonymous Story" and "Big Volodya and Little Volodya."

1894.   Second trip to Italy and to Paris. Health worsens. Publishes "The Student," "Rothschild's Fiddle," "The Head Gardener's Story," "The Literature Teacher," "The Black Monk," and "At a Country House."

Alexander III dies and is succeeded by his son, the conservative and vacillating Nicholas II.

1895.   *The Island of Sakhalin* published. Chekhov meets Lev Tolstoy at his estate Yasnaya Polyana.

Chekhov writes *The Seagull*, publishes "Three Years," "Ariadne," "His Wife," "Whitebrow," "Murder," and "Anna Round the Neck."

1896.   Chekhov sponsors the construction of a primary school in the village of Talezh. Serial publication of "My Life" and "The House with a Mansard."

October 17. The premiere of *The Seagull* at the Alexandra

Theatre in St. Petersburg fails. Chekhov flees during the second act.

October 21. Relative success of the play at its second performance.

1896–1897. Strikes of factory workers lead to a law limiting adult work to eleven and a half hours a day.

1897. The first All-Russian Congress of Stage Workers meets in Moscow to argue questions of trade conditions and artistic principles.

Stanislavsky and Nemirovich-Danchenko found the Moscow Art Theatre.

Chekhov sponsors the construction of a primary school in the village of Novosyolky. Participates in the All-Russian census of the population. Father dies.

March–April. Hospitalized with first acute attack of pulmonary tuberculosis. Reads Maurice Maeterlinck.

September. Travels to France for medical treatment.

Uncle Vanya, Ivanov, The Seagull, and one-act plays published, as well as stories "Peasants," "The Savage," "At Home," and "In the Cart."

1898. Thirteen thousand students at Moscow University go on strike to protest repressive moves on the part of the administration; orders are given to enlist them in the army.

May. Chekhov returns from abroad. Relations with Suvorin strained in connection with the Dreyfus trial.

September. Settles in Yalta after suffering a pulmonary hemorrhage. Publishes the stories "Calling on Friends," "Gooseberries," "About Love," "A Case History," and "Ionych."

December 17. The Seagull, staged by Stanislavsky, is revived with great success at the Moscow Art Theatre.

1899. Theatres in Kiev, Kharkov, and Nizhny Novgorod play *Uncle Vanya*. Chekhov decides to turn it into a short novel, but does not. Offered to the Maly, *Uncle Vanya* is considered offensive to professors and is turned down.

Tolstoy's *Resurrection* and Gorky's *Foma Gordeev* published.

Chekhov attends a performance of *The Seagull* in Yalta. Sells all rights to his works to the publisher A. F. Marks for 75,000 rubles (in current purchasing power, approximately $81,000). Begins to edit his complete works. Awarded Order of St. Stanislas, second class, for work in education. Publishes "On Official Business," "Lady with Lapdog," "The Darling," and "The New Villa."

June. Sells his estate in Melikhovo. Has a house built in Yalta.

October 26. Premiere of *Uncle Vanya* at the Art Theatre.

1900. *January.* Elected to honorary membership in the Literary division of the Academy of Sciences. Publishes "In the Ravine" and "At Christmas."

April. The Art Theatre plays *Uncle Vanya* and *The Seagull* in Sevastopol, in the presence of the author.

August–December. Writes *Three Sisters.* Finishes the play in Nice.

1901. *January–February.* Trip to Italy.

January 31. Premiere of *Three Sisters* at the Moscow Art Theatre with considerable success.

May 25. Marries the actress Olga Knipper, who plays Masha.

The Marxist journal *Life*, which publishes Gorky, is banned. Gorky is expelled from Nizhny Novgorod.

1902.   Chekhov publishes "The Bishop." Complete works published in eleven volumes. Awarded Griboedov Prize of Society of Dramatic Authors and Opera Composers for *Three Sisters*. Begins *The Cherry Orchard*.

March. Olga Knipper suffers miscarriage.

August. Resigns in protest from the Academy of Sciences when Gorky's election is nullified at the tsar's behest.

Gorky writes *The Lower Depths*.

1903.   At a Congress in London, the Social Democratic Workingman's Party is taken over by the radical Bolshevist wing, led by Vladimir Lenin.

Second edition of Chekhov's complete works published in sixteen volumes.

Publishes his last story, "Betrothed," in the magazine *Everybody's*.

June. The censor rules that his plays cannot be performed in people's theaters, low-priced theater for the working class.

September. The Cherry Orchard is finished. Nemirovich-Danchenko and Stanislavsky are enthusiastic. Chekhov attends rehearsals.

An atrocious pogrom occurs in Kishinyov, with 47 dead and 2,000 families ruined.

1904. Chekhov's health deteriorates.

January 14 or 15. Attends a rehearsal of *The Cherry Orchard.*

January 17. Premiere at the Art Theatre, where a celebration in his honor is held.

Spring. A new, grave attack of tuberculosis.

April 2. First performance of *Orchard* in St. Petersburg a great success, greater than in Moscow, according to Nemirovich and Stanislavsky.

June 1. Publication of the play in a separate edition by Marks.

June 3. Departure for Germany with Olga Knipper.

July 2/15. Dies in Badenweiler.

July 9/22. Buried in Novo-devichy cemetery in Moscow.

The Mensheviks drive the Bolsheviks from the Central Committee of the Social Democratic Working-man's Party, but drop out the following year, leaving the field to the Bolsheviks.

The Russo-Japanese war breaks out.

1909. First performance of a Chekhov play in English: *The Seagull,* translated by George Calderon, at the Glasgow Repertory Theatre.

A NOTE ON THE TRANSLATION

The text on which this translation is based is that in A. P. Chekhov, *Polnoe sobranie sochineniy i pisem v tridtsati tomakh* (*Complete Works and Letters in Thirty Volumes*), edited by N. F. Belchikov et al. (Moscow: Nauka, 1974–1984). The Russian text was drawn from the latest version published in Chekhov's lifetime and subject to his revision.

Chekhov had his doubts about the efficacy of translation, and after reading some Russian prose translated into French, concluded that transmission of Russian literature into another language was pointless. Later, when his own plays began to be translated, he lamented that purely Russian phenomena would have no meaning for foreign audiences. To offset these misgivings, the translator of Chekhov must be as sedulous in making choices as the author was in composing the original work.

From his earliest farces, Chekhov wrote plays with an eye to their being performed. He often had specific actors in mind, and, despite his discomfort with histrionic convention, he expected his dialogue to be recited from the stage. Therefore, translating his plays entails problems different from those encountered in translating his prose fiction. At first sight, the vocabulary and sentence structure seem straightforward enough. Under scrutiny, however, the seeming simplicity turns out to be illusory.

The literary psychoanalyst Gregory Zilboorg, initiating American readers into Russian drama in 1920, stated point-blank that Chekhov was fundamentally untranslatable, more so even than Aleksandr Ostrovsky and Maksim Gorky. "Chekhov's plays lose their chief element in translation into whatever other language: the particular harmony and rhythm of the original. The student must bear in mind that studying Chekhov's drama in English he actually studies only some elements of them, the rest being lost in a foreign language."[1]

The "harmony and rhythm" so lost derive from a number of sources. First, Chekhov uses language to consolidate his major plays: recurrent phrases echo off one another, often for ironic effect. George Bernard Shaw was another playwright well aware that it was precisely this adhesive repetition of key words that knit a play together. He scolded his German translator,

> The way in which you translate every word just as it comes and then forget it and translate it some other way when it begins (or should begin) to make the audience laugh, is enough to whiten the hair on an author's head. Have you ever read Shakespear's Much Ado About Nothing? In it a man calls a constable an ass, and throughout the rest of the play the constable can think of nothing but this insult and keeps on saying, "But forget not, mas-

ters, that I am an ass." Now if you translated Much Ado, you would make the man call the constable a Schaffkopf. On the next page he would be a Narr, then a Maul, then a Thier, and perhaps the very last time an Esel.[2]

This was such a salient principle for Shaw that he hammered at it the following month: "I tell you again and again most earnestly and seriously, that unless you repeat the words that I have repeated, you will throw away all the best stage effects and make the play unpopular with the actors . . . Half the art of dialogue consists in the echoing of words—the tossing back & forwards of phrases from one to another like a cricket ball . . ."[3]

What is true for Shaw is equally true for Chekhov. In Chekhov, a commonplace uttered in the first act may return to resonate with fresh significance. Medvedenko's "It gets you going around in circles," uttered early on as a response to his financial straits, is quoted in the last act by Dr. Dorn to mock him. Masha's second-act insistence that her love must be uprooted from her heart rings all the more hollow when repeated in Act Four, after her marriage.

Lexical and etymological elements subliminally affect the atmosphere. Literary allusions to the Russian classics (Pushkin, Gogol, Ostrovsky) enrich the cultural context. For the educated Russian of Chekhov's time, they would have been immediately familiar. However, the translator must be alert to what I call embedded quotations, less obvious than explicit citations from literature. At the play's end, Nina remarks that both she and Treplyov have fallen into the *omut*, usually translated as "whirlpool" or "maelstrom." But earlier Treplyov had alluded to Nina as he mentioned Pushkin's unfinished verse play *Rusalka* in which the abandoned miller's daughter drowns herself in the millrace (also *omut*) and turns into a water-nymph. In context, "millrace" is the correct translation, but that would mean nothing, even to a modern Russian audience. So "maelstrom" is preferable.

In his last plays, Chekhov is extremely careful in choosing his words. A French translator has pointed out that in *The Seagull*, Chekhov employed three separate words for *why*: *otchego*, *zachem*, and *pochemu*. I have been very careful to observe those choices, translating them as "how come," "what for" and "why," respectively. Hence, in this translation the famous opening line is not "Why do you always wear black?" but "How come you always wear black?," which distinguishes Medvedenko's way of asking a question from that of others.

Every character in Chekhov speaks in a particular cadence and with a particular vocabulary. Sorin's catchphrase, "When all's said and done" (*v kontse kontsov*), is an obvious example; less blatant is Trigorin's regular mention of elements of a literary life—proofreading, editorial offices, theatre audiences. When the country girl Nina starts using technical theatrical lingo (she describes Konstantin's play as a *chitka*, or readthrough), we realize she has been paying close attention to Arkadina.

Harder to pin down is the "specific gravity" of a statement that may reside in its structure. Russian can reassemble the elements of a sentence to make a particular emphasis; English has to find a way of reproducing this. Mere phrasebook translation, offering a direct statement, can betray the subtle emphases of the original.

Finally, certain words and phrases that once held a special meaning may require that an explanation be embedded in the translation, particularly if it is meant to be performed. The quotations from Nekrasov's poems have to reflect the pseudo-progressivism of the person doing the quoting. Who is the unpronounceable Poprishchin referred to in a speech of Trigorin's? Just what is the food at the railway station buffets that he objects to? (*Kotlety* are not "cutlets," as most translators have it, but fried meat patties. He's complaining about greasy fast food made of unidentifiable ingredients.)

The same applies to jokes. Chekhov often embeds *jeux de mots* and facetious phrasing as depth charges; the translator's first task is to be aware of them, the second to find a way of making them detonate properly.

These particularities of Chekhov come in addition to the usual problems experienced in translating from Russian: the passive constructions, the distinction between verbs of imperfect and perfect action (the difference between *strelilsya* and *zastrelilsya*, Konstantin's having shot himself and having shot himself for good), and onomatopoeic sounds that are overlooked or scanted. In the symbolist play in Act One, the refrain *"Kholodno, kholodno, kholodno. Pusto, pusto, pusto. Uzhasno, uzhasno, uzhasno"* can be literally translated, as is usually the case, "Cold, cold, cold. Empty, empty, empty. Horrible, horrible, horrible." This misses the ritual repetition of the adverbial ending *o* and Konstantin's attempt to sound like a symbolist poet. My solution is: "Chilly, chilly, chilly. Empty, empty, empty. Ghastly, ghastly, ghastly."

"The shock of the new" in Chekhov's handling of dialogue contributed mightily to his reputation in his lifetime, but today tends to be lost or overlooked. As Nils Åke Nilsson pointed out, Chekhov is an unacknowledged precursor of the Futurists and their launching of a *zaumny*, or transrational language. He cites as examples the phrase "You've Gavril-ed it up enough" in *Ivanov*, the trom-tom-tom exchange in *Three Sisters*, and Gaev's billiard jargon in *The Cherry Orchard*, calling this a "new dramatic syntax."[4] He might also have cited Chekhov's imitation of symbolist rhetoric in Konstantin's play in *The Seagull*.

The American critic Stark Young, when he set out to translate *The Seagull* for the Lunts in 1938, singled out "those balances, repetitions for stage effect, repetitions for stage economy, theatrical combinations and devices, time-patterns, and so on, that are the fruits of much intention and technical craft, and that are almost totally absent from the translation.[5] Yet even he trembled before Chekhov's linguistic audacity: "Chekhov's dialogue is perhaps a trifle more colloquial than mine. Certainly it is more colloquial than I should ever dare to be; for in a translation any very marked colloquialism is always apt to hurt the economy of effect by raising questions as to what the original could have been to come out so patly as that."[6]

Young took as an example Trigorin's remark that when he gets a whiff of heliotrope *skoree motayu na us*, literally "quickly I wrap it around my moustache." Any good Russian dictionary will tell you that this is a figure of speech meaning "I make a mental note of something." Perhaps, as Young feared, it is as wrong to translate this literally as it might be to translate "he got my goat" literally into Russian. Nevertheless, to translate it as he does— "Quickly I make note of it"—is to substitute the bland for the colorful. My own solution, bearing in mind first Chekhov's fascination with facial hair (every one of his major plays contains remarks about whiskers) and next that Trigorin is an avid fisherman, is "I instantly reel it in on my moustache." His following phrase, *Lovlyu v sebya i vas na kazhdoy fraze,* Young renders awkwardly as "Every sentence, every word I say and you say, I lie in wait for it." However, it ought to continue the piscatorial imagery, since Chekhov may have had in the mind the Biblical idiom, to fish in troubled waters, in Russian *lovit' rybu v mutnoy vode.* It helps to know that from his long boyhood experience as a chorister under his father's tutelage, Chekhov's mind was well-stocked with Scriptural commonplaces. My solution goes "I'm angling in myself and you for every phrase."

Young was very cautious in rendering the jokiness of Chekhov's dialogue and sought a simplicity that denatures the special flavor of the language. In this respect, Chekhov is very deceptive. His lexical choices and often straightforward syntax enable him to be used in the classroom, but this seeming simplicity overlies a deliberate restriction of vocabulary. Consequently, unusual words and phrases stand out all the more. In addition, the sentence structure is organized poetically in order to express character and, as an actor of the time would put it, make points. Translators, led astray by Chekhov's poker-faced approach (in some respects similar to Mark Twain's), have often made him sound more wooden and monotonous, less fruity and lyrical, than he is.

Finally, I have not tried to pretend that Chekhov is anything other than Russian. Although I have converted weights and measures into Western equivalents so that an audience can more easily gauge distances and density, I have left currency, beverages, and, in particular, names in their Russian forms. Modern readers and audiences rapidly adjust to patronymics, diminutives, and nicknames. If one is to turn Pyotr into Peter and Masha into Mary, then one must go the whole hog and refer to Connie instead of Kostya and, to be consistent, *Uncle Vanya* as *Uncle Jack*.

NOTES

1 Gregory Zilboorg, "A course in Russian drama," *The Drama* (Nov. 1920): 69.

2 *Bernard Shaw's Letters to Siegfried Trebitsch*, ed. Samuel A. Weiss (Stanford: Stanford University Press, 1986), p. 30 (26 Dec. 1902). The words translate as "sheep's head," "fool," "muzzle," "beast," "ass."

3 Ibid., 15 Jan. 1903, p. 36.

4 Nils Åke Nilsson, "Two Chekhovs: Mayakovskiy on Chekhov's 'futurism,'" in Jean-Pierre Barricelli, ed., *Chekhov's Great Plays: A Critical Anthology* (New York: New York University Press, 1981), pp. 251–61.

5 Stark Young, "Translating *The Sea Gull*," in *The Sea Gull, A Drama in Four Acts*, translated from the Russian of Anton Chekhov by Stark Young (New York: Samuel French, 1950), pp. xii–xv.

6 Ibid., p. xix.

PRONUNCIATION GUIDE

Irina Nikolaevna Arkadina *ee-REE-nah nee-kah-LYE-eff-nah ahr-KAH-dee-nah*

Konstantin Gavrilovich Treplyov *kahn-stahn-TEEN gahv-REEL-ah-veech Trip-LYAWF*

Kostya *KAWST-yah*

Gavrilych *gahv-REEL-ihch*

Pyotr Nikolaevich Sorin *PYAW-tr nee-kah-LYE-yeh-veech SAW-reen*

Petrushka *pit-ROO-shash*

Nina Mikhailovna Zarechnaya *NEE-nah mee-'HEIL-ahf-nah zah-RYECH-nye-ah*

Ilya Afanasevich Shamraev *eel-YAH ah-fah-NAHSS-yeh-veech shahm-RY-eff*

Polina Andreevna *pah-LEE-nah ahn-DRAY-eff-nah*

Marya Ilyinishna *MAHR-ya eel-YEEN-eesh-nah*

Masha *MAH-shah*

Mashenka *MAH-shin-kah*

Boris Alekseevich Trigorin *bah-REESS ah-lik-SAY-eh-veech tree-GAWR-een*

Evgeny Sergeevich Dorn *yihv-GHEHN-ee sehr-GAY-eh-veech DAWRN*

Semyon Semyonovich Medvedenko *sim-YAWN sim-YAWN-ah-veech myehd-VYEHD-in-kah*

Yasha *YAH-shah*

Odessa *ah-DYEHSS-ah*

Nekrasov *nik-RAHSS-ahff*

Duse *DOO-zah*

Pavel Semyonych Chadin *PAH-wehl sim-YAWN-eech CHAH-deen*

Rasplyuev *rahss-PLYOO-yehf*

Sadovsky *sah-DAWF-skee*

Tolstoy *tahl-STOY*

Turgenev *toor-GHEHN-yehf*

Suzdaltsev *sooz-DAHL-tsehf*

Elizavetgrad *ill-EEZ-ah-vyeht-grahd*

Izmailov *eez-MY-lahf*

Matryona *math-RYAW-nah*

Pushkin *POOSH-keen*

Kharkov *'HAHR-kahf*

Yelets *yell-YEHTS*

INTRODUCTION

The first production of *The Seagull*, at the Alexandra Theatre in St. Petersburg on October 17, 1896, has come down in theatrical legend as a classic fiasco. This is an exaggeration, however. The cast was a strong one, with Vladimir Davydov, who had created the title role in Chekhov's first produced play, *Ivanov*, as Sorin and the luminous Vera Kommissarzhevskaya as Nina. During the scant week of rehearsals, Chekhov was in attendance, prompting the actors and correcting the director. Like most sensitive playwrights, he was dismayed by wasted time and the actors' predilection for superficial characterizations that stunted his brain-children, but by the last rehearsals his expectations had risen.

These were dashed on opening night, for the spectators had come with expectations of their own, hoping to see their favorite comedienne Levkeeva, whose benefit performance it was. They laughed, booed, and whistled at whatever struck them as funny, from Nina's soliloquy to Treplyov's entrance with the dead gull, to the actors' ad-libs when they went up in their lines. Chekhov fled the theater, vowing never again to write for the stage. Nevertheless, the ensuing performances, with the actors more secure, played to respectful houses. Before *The Seagull* closed in November, it had become a *succès d'estime*, with Kommissarzhevskaya proclaimed as brilliant. It was successfully revived in Kiev, Taganrog, and other provincial centers, providing Chekhov with handsome royalties.

The writer Nemirovich-Danchenko, an admirer of the play, thought *The Seagull* was just the thing to rescue the flagging fortunes of his newly founded Moscow Art Theatre, whose first season was in danger of bankruptcy. Nemirovich pressed it upon his reluctant colleague Stanislavsky, who at first found the play incomprehensible and unsympathetic. Stanislavsky retired to his country estate to compose a directorial score, which he sent piecemeal to Moscow, where Nemirovich was rehearsing the actors.

Stanislavsky's fundamental approach to staging *The Seagull* differed little from his direction of historical drama. He sought in contemporary Russian life the same picturesque groupings, the same telling mannerisms, the same pregnant pauses that had enthralled audiences when he reconstructed seventeenth-century Muscovy or Renaissance Venice. Rather than inquiring into Chekhov's intentions, Stanislavsky took the play as romantic melodrama: Nina was an innocent ruined by that "scoundrelly Lovelace" Trigorin, and Treplyov was a misunderstood Byronic genius, the hero of the piece. Nor, at this stage of his development, did Stanislavsky try organically to elicit performances from the actors. Their every move, reaction, and intonation were prescribed by his score and learned by rote.

The opening night, December 17, 1898, despite offstage jitters, was a palpable hit, insuring the theater's success, and *The Seagull* became the Moscow Art Theatre's trademark. Chekhov was less than ecstatic. He thought that Stanislavsky misinterpreted Trigorin by making him too elegant and formal; he detested Mariya Roksanova's ladylike Nina. Whatever his misgivings, the educated, middle-class audiences took to the play precisely because, for the first time, "the way we live now" was subjected to the same careful counterfeit presentment that had hitherto been applied only to the exotic past. The spectators beheld their own tics and heard their own speech patterns meticulously copied.

Taking advantage of the outdoor settings of the early acts and the dimly lit interior at the end, Stanislavsky laid on climatic and atmospheric effects to create an overpowering mood (*nastroenie*). The method, relying on sound effects, diffused lighting, and a snail's pace, worked so well for *The Seagull* that it became standard operating procedure at the Art Theatre for Chekhov's later plays and, indeed, those of almost any author. In the last analysis, it was the pervasive mood that made *The Seagull* a hit. The young actor Meyerhold, who played Treplyov, later credited Stanislavsky with being the first to link the sound of rain on the window and morning light peeping through the shutters with the characters' behavior. "At that time this was a discovery."[1] The dramatist Leonid Andreev was to call it "panpsychism," the animation of everything in a Chekhov play from distant music to the chirp of a cricket to munching an apple, each contributing equally to the play's total effect.[2]

Chekhov's objections to the Moscow interpretation did not, however, spring from its style, but from the imbalance in meaning that Stanislavsky had induced. Although it contains what Chekhov called "a ton of love," *The Seagull* is not a soap opera about triangular relationships or a romantic dramatization of Trigorin's "subject for a short story." It is perhaps Chekhov's most personal play in its treatment of the artist's *métier*. The theme of splendors and miseries of artists is plainly struck by Medvedenko at the start, when he enviously refers to Nina and Treplyov sharing in a creative endeavor. Nina picks it up when she explains why her parents won't let her come to Sorin's estate: "They say this place is Bohemia." Years of theater-going, reviewing, dealing with performers and managers were distilled by Chekhov into a density of metaphor for the artistic experience, for the contrasts between commercialism and idealism, facility and aspiration, purposeless talent and diligent mediocrity. Of the central characters, one is a would-be playwright, another a successful author; one is an acclaimed if second-rate star of the footlights, another an aspiring actress.

Stanislavsky's black-and-white vision of the play also contradicted Chekhov's attempt to create multiple heroes and multiple conflicts. Treplyov seems the protagonist because the play begins with his artistic credo and his moment of revolt, and it ends with his self-destruction. In terms of stage time, however, he shares the limelight with many other claimants, whose ambitions cancel out one another.

Nina, similarly, cannot be singled out as the one survivor who preserves her ideals in spite of all. The type of the victimized young girl, abandoned by her love and coming to a bad end, recurred in Russian literature from N. M. Karamzin's *Poor Liza*

(1792) onward. Often, she was depicted as the ward of an old woman who, in her cruelty or wilful egoism, promotes the girl's downfall. Many plays of Ostrovsky and Aleksey Potekhin feature such a pair, and the relationship is subtly handled by Turgenev in *A Month in the Country* (1850). In *The Seagull*, the relationship is rarefied: It is Arkadina's example, rather than her intention, that sends Nina to Moscow, maternity, and mumming.

Chekhov's early stories abound with actresses who lead erratic lives and endure slurs and contempt for it, but Nina continues to dismiss the shoddiness of the work she is given, determined to develop an inner strength, regardless of old forms or new. Should she be extolled as a shining talent to be contrasted with Arkadina's *routinier* activity? Nina's ideas on art and fame are jejune and couched in the bromides of cheap fiction; her inability to see Treplyov's play as other than words and speeches, her offer to eat black bread and live in a garret for the reward of celebrity, are obtuse and juvenile. Hers are not dreams that deserve to be realized, and there is nothing tragic in her having to reconcile them with the ordinary demands of life.

Similarly, Chekhov does not mean us to accept at face value Treplyov's harsh verdicts on his mother and her lover. They may truckle to popular demand, but they are crippled by self-doubt. Arkadina, barnstorming the countryside in the Russian equivalent of *East Lynne*, is convinced that she is performing a public service; her stage name ambivalently refers both to Arcadia and to a garish amusement park in St. Petersburg. Trigorin, well aware that he is falling short of his masters Tolstoy and Turgenev, still plugs away in the tradition of well-observed realism.

Treplyov and Trigorin cannot be set up as hostile antitheses; as Chudakov says, they "themselves call their basic theses into question."[3] Treplyov's desire for new forms is a more vociferous and less knowing version of Trigorin's self-deprecation. The younger writer scorns the elder as a hack, but by the play's end, he is longing to find formulas for his own writing. Arkadina may not have read her son's story and Trigorin may not have cut the pages on any story but his own, but Treplyov himself admits he has never read Trigorin's stuff, thus partaking of their casual egoism. Since both Treplyov and Trigorin contain elements of Chekhov, a more productive antithesis might be that of idealism and materialism, with Treplyov the romantic at one end and the schoolmaster Medvedenko at the other. The two men are linked by Masha, who loves the one and barely puts up with the other. Each act opens with her statement of the hopelessness of her situation. Even here, though, the antithesis is not complete: Treplyov is as hamstrung by his poverty as Medvedenko, and the teacher cherishes his own wishes to make art with a beloved object.

The literary critic Prince Mirsky pointed out that *bezdarnost* ("lack of talent") was a "characteristically Chekhovian word"[4] in its absence of positive qualities. Chekhov described talent to Suvorin as the ability "to distinguish important evidence from unimportant" (May 30, 1888). In *The Seagull*, "talent" is the touchstone by which the characters evaluate themselves and one another. Treplyov fears "he has no talent at all," but he rebukes Nina for considering him a "mediocrity, a nonentity" and points sarcastically to Trigorin as the "genuine talent." In her anger,

Arkadina lashes out at her son by referring to "people with no talent but plenty of pretensions," to which he retaliates, "I'm more talented than the lot of you put together." In Act One, Arkadina encourages Nina to go on stage by saying, "You must have talent," and in the last act, Treplyov grudgingly acknowledges that "she showed some talent at screaming or dying." Trigorin complains that his public regards him as no more than "charming and talented," yet when Arkadina caresses him with "You're so talented," he succumbs to her blandishments.

The point is that "talent" exists independently of human relations and can be consummated in isolation. To be talented is not necessarily to be a superior person. As usual, Dr. Dorn sees most acutely to the heart of the matter: "You're a talented fellow," he tells Treplyov, "but without a well-defined goal . . . your talent will destroy you." Tactlessly, in Arkadina's presence, he declares, "there aren't many brilliant talents around these days . . . but the average actor has improved greatly"; sharing Chekhov's distrust of the grand gesture, he prefers a betterment of the general lot to artistic supermen. Even Nina finally realizes that fame and glamour are less important than staying power.

Treplyov's display of talent, his symbolist play located in a void where all things are extinct and the only conflicts are between the Universal Will and the Principle of Eternal Matter, may seem like parody. Chekhov, however, is careful to place the harsh criticism on the lips of Arkadina, whose taste and motives are suspect, and Nina, who is parroting actor's jargon she has heard from her. Chekhov is not ridiculing Treplyov for his espousal of a new form but for his inability to preserve the purity of his ideal: His symbolist venture is a garble of popular stage techniques incongruous with his poetic aspirations, "Curtain, downstage, upstage, and beyond that, empty space," "special effects." He seems unable to find an original play to express his nebulous ideas; his play, as Chekhov said to Suvorin of the Norwegian Bjørnson's *Beyond Human Power*, "has no meaning because the idea isn't clear. It's impossible to have one's characters perform miracles, when you yourself have no sharply defined conviction as to miracles" (June 20, 1896). In his notebooks, Chekhov stipulated, "Treplyov has no fixed goals, and that's what destroyed him. Talent destroyed him."

Chekhov, for his part, did manage to initiate his own new form in The Seagull, inchoate and transitional though it may be. For the first time, he did away with "French scenes," allowing each act to develop not through the entrances and exits of characters but by a concealed inner dynamic. The overall rhythm of the play is also carefully scored. As he told Suvorin on November 21, 1895, "I wrote it forte and ended it pianissimo, contrary to all the rules of dramatic art." The forte passages occur in the first three acts, which are compressed into a week's time; then there is a lapse of two years before the pianissimo of Act Four. The characters must fill in this long gap in their own knowledge by the awkward device of asking one another what's been going on. But this is the result of Chekhov's eagerness to keep offstage what a traditional playwright would have saved for his obligatory scenes. The most intense and sensational actions—Nina's seduction and abandonment, the death of her child, Trigorin's return to Arkadina—are, like Treplyov's two suicide attempts, left to our imagination. We are allowed to see the antecedents and the consequences, but not the act itself.

The two-year hiatus between the third and fourth acts stresses the recurrent theme of memory. The past is always idyllic: Arkadina's reminiscence of life along the lakeshore, Poling's evocation of her past fling with the Doctor, Shamraev's evocation of antediluvian actors, Sorin's rosy picture of an urban existence are the older generation's forecast of the clashing recollections of Treplyov and Nina. With wry irony, Chekhov divulges each of his characters' insensitivity or obliviousness. "It's too late," insists Dorn, when Polina tries to rekindle their earlier affair. "I don't remember," shrugs Arkadina, when her charitable behavior is recalled. "Don't remember," says Trigorin, when he is shown the gull he had stuffed in memory of his first conversation with Nina.

Another new form that Chekhov initiated in *The Seagull* is the emblematic progression of localities. The first act is set in "a portion of the park on Sorin's estate," where the path to the lake is blocked off by Treplyov's trestle stage. This particular region is remote from the main house, and Treplyov has chosen it as his private turf: The characters who make up his audience must enter his world of shadows and dampness. They spend only a brief time there before returning to the safe norms evoked by the strains of the piano drifting into the clearing. Treplyov wants his work of art to be seen as coexistent with nature, with what Dorn calls "the spellbinding lake." Ironically, his manmade stage prevents people from walking to the lake, which his mother equates with "laughter, noise, gunshots, and one romance after another," the ordinary recreations Treplyov disdains. The most casual response to the lake comes from Trigorin, who sees it simply as a place to fish.

Act Two moves to Arkadina's territory, a house with a large veranda. The lake can now be seen in the bright sunlight, not the pallid moonshine. The surrounding verdure is a "croquet lawn," as manicured and well-kempt as Arkadina herself, who keeps "up to the mark . . . my hair done *comme il faut*." Notably, Treplyov is the only member of the family circle who does not go into the house in this act. It stands for his mother's hold on life, and from its depths comes the call that keeps Trigorin on the estate.

The dining room of Act Three brings us into the house, but it is a neutral space, used for solitary meals, wound-dressing, farewells. The act is organized as a series of tête-à-têtes that are all the more intense for taking place in a somewhere no one can call his own. The last act takes place in a drawing room that Treplyov has turned into a workroom. As the act opens, preparations are being made to convert it into a sickroom. The huddling together of the dying Sorin and the artistically moribund Treplyov implies that they are both "the man who wanted" but who never got what he wanted: a wife and a literary career. Once again, Treplyov has tried to set up a space of his own, only to have it overrun by a bustling form of life that expels him to the margins. To have a moment alone with Nina, he must bar the door to the dining room with a chair; the moment he removes the impediment, the intruders fill his space, turning it into a game room. His private act of suicide must occur elsewhere.

This final locale has a Maeterlinckian tinge, for there is a glass door through which Nina enters, romantically draped in a *talma*, an enveloping cloak named after Napoleon's favorite tragedian. After days spent wandering around the lake, she emerges from an aperture no other character uses, to come in from "the garden," where "it's dark . . . that stage . . . stands bare and unsightly, like a skeleton, and the scene curtain flaps in the wind." The plays of Belgian poet Maurice Maeterlinck, whom Chekhov greatly admired, are full of mysterious windows and doors that serve as entries into another world, beyond which invisible forces are to be intuited and uncanny figures glimpsed. Quoting Turgenev, Nina identifies herself as a "homeless wanderer, seeking a haven." But what is "warm and cozy" to her is claustrophobic and stifling to Treplyov.

In fact, the whole estate is an enclosure for the characters' frustration. This is no Turgenevian nest of gentry, for none of the characters feels at home here. Arkadina would rather be in a hotel room learning lines; Sorin would like to be in his office, hearing street noise. Seeing his nephew withering away on the estate, he tries to pry loose some money for a trip abroad. Nina's are always flying visits, time snatched from her oppressed life elsewhere. Medvedenko is there on sufferance. Shamraev the overseer is a retired military man with no skills as a farm manager. Only Trigorin is loath to depart, because, for him, the estate provides enforced idleness. The lake's enchantment can be felt as the spell of Sleeping Beauty's castle. Everyone who sets foot there is suspended in time, frozen in place. Real life seems to go on somewhere else.

This symbolic use of environment is better integrated than the more obvious symbol of the seagull. In Ibsen's *The Wild*

Duck, the title is of essential importance: All the leading charac-ters are defined by their attitude to the bird, and it exists, unseen, as they re-create it in their private mythologies. The seagull, however, has significance for only three characters: Treplyov, who employs it as a symbol; Trigorin, who reinterprets its sym-bolic meaning; and Nina, who adopts and eventually repudiates the symbolism. For Treplyov, it is a means of turning art into life: Feeling despised and rejected, he shoots the bird as a surrogate and, when the surrogate is in turn rejected, shoots himself. Nina had felt "lured to the lake like a gull" but will not accept Trep-lyov's bird imagery for his self-identification. However, when her idol Trigorin spins his yarn about a girl who lives beside a lake, happy and free as a gull, she avidly adopts the persona, even though his notion of her freedom is wholly inaccurate. The story turns out to be false, for the man who ruined the bird is not the one who ruins the girl. Nor is Nina ruined in any real sense. She starts to sign her letters to Treplyov "The Seagull" (or "A Seagull"—Russian has no definite articles); he links this with the mad miller in Pushkin's poem *The Rusalka*, who insanely thought himself a crow after his daughter, seduced and aban-doned, drowned herself. Both Treplyov and Trigorin try to recast Nina as a fictional character, the conventional ruined girl who takes her own life. In the last act, however, she refuses this iden-tity: "I'm a seagull. No, not that," spurning both Treplyov's martyr-bird and Trigorin's novelletish heroine. She survives, if only in an anti-romantic, workaday world. Ultimately, Chekhov pre-fers the active responsibilities contingent on accepting one's lot, even if this means a fate like Nina's.

NOTES

1 A. G. Gladkov, "Meyerhold govorit," *Novy Mir* 8 (1961): 221.

2 Leonid Andreev, "Letters on the Theatre," in *Russian Dramatic Theory from Pushkin to the Symbolists*, ed. and trans. L. Senelick (Austin: University of Texas Press, 1981), pp. 238–242.

3 A. P. Chudakov, Chekhov's *Poetics*, trans. F. J. Cruise and D. Dragt (Ann Arbor: Ardis, 1983), p. 193.

4 D. S. Mirsky, *Contemporary Russian Literature 1881–1925* (London: George Routledge and Sons, 1926), p. 88.

THE SEAGULL[1]

Чайка

A Comedy in Four Acts

CAST

ARKADINA,[2] **IRINA NIKOLAEVNA,** *married name Treplyova, actress*

TREPLYOV,[3] **KONSTANTIN GAVRILOVICH,** *her son, a young man*

---

1 Why do *sea*gulls hover over an inland lake on Sorin's estate? In Russian, *chaika* is simply a gull. *Sea* has the connotation of distance and freedom, quite out of keeping with this play. In English, however, *The Seagull* has gained common currency as the play's title, so I have retained it here, but refer simply to the "gull" in the text.

2 Ivan Bunin complained that Chekhov gave the women in his plays names befitting provincial actresses, but since two of the women in *The Seagull* are provincial actresses, no great harm is done. Arkadina is a stage name based on *Arcadia*, with its promise of a blissful pastoral existence (the sort of boring country life Arkadina loathes); but Arcadia was also the name of a garish amusement park in Moscow.

3 *Treplyov* hints at *trepat*, to be disorganized or feverish, *trepach*, an idle chatterbox, and *trepetat*, to quiver or palpitate.

SORIN,[4] PYOTR NIKOLAEVICH, *her brother*

NINA MIKHAILOVNA ZARECHNAYA,[5] *a young woman, daughter of a wealthy landowner*

SHAMRAEV, ILYA AFANASEVICH, *retired lieutenant, overseer of Sorin's estate*

POLINA ANDREEVNA, *his wife*

MASHA, *his daughter*

TRIGORIN, BORIS ALEKSEEVICH, *a man of letters*

DORN, EVGENY SERGEEVICH, *a doctor of medicine*

MEDVEDENKO,[6] SEMYON SEMYONOVICH, *a schoolteacher*

YAKOV, *a workman*

A COOK

A HOUSEMAID

The action takes place on Sorin's country estate. Between Acts Three and Four two years elapse.

---

4 *Sorin* seems to come from *sorit*, to mess things up, and is indicative of the old man's habitually rumpled state.

5 *Zarechnaya* means "across the river" and suggests Nina's dwelling on the opposite side of the lake, as well as her alien spirit in the world of Sorin's estate.

6 *Medved* means bear, and the name's ending suggests a Ukrainian origin.

ACT ONE

*A section of the park on Sorin's estate. A wide pathway
leading from the audience upstage into the park and
toward a lake is blocked by a platform, hurriedly
slapped together for an amateur theatrical, so that
the lake is completely obscured. Bushes to the left and
right of the platform. A few chairs, a small table. The
sun has just gone down. On the platform, behind the
lowered curtain, are YAKOV and other workmen; we
can hear them coughing and hammering. MASHA
and MEDVEDENKO enter left, on their way back
from a walk.*

MEDVEDENKO. How come you always wear black?

MASHA. I'm in mourning for my life. I'm unhappy.

MEDVEDENKO. But how come? (*Thinking about it.*) I don't get
it . . . You're healthy, and that father of yours may not be rich,
but he's doing all right. My life's a lot tougher than yours. All I
make is twenty-three rubles a month, not counting deductions,[7]
but you don't see me in mourning.

They sit down.

MASHA. It's got nothing to do with money. Even a poor person
can be happy.

---

7 A voluntary contribution from one's monthly salary toward an old-age pension.

MEDVEDENKO. In theory, but in reality it doesn't work that way; there's me and my mother and two sisters and my little brother, and my pay comes to twenty-three rubles. Got to buy food and drink, don't you? And tea and sugar? And tobacco?. It gets you going in circles.

MASHA (*looking round at the platform*). The show will be starting soon.

MEDVEDENKO. Yes. Miss Zarechnaya is going to act in a play written by Konstantin Gavrilovich. They're in love, and today their souls will merge in an attempt to present a joint artistic creation. But my soul and yours have no mutual points of convergence. I love you, my longing for you drives me out of the house, every day I walk four miles here and four miles back and all I ever get from you is indifferentism.[8] No wonder. I've got no money and lots of dependents . . . . Who wants to marry a man who can't support himself?

MASHA. Don't be silly. (*Takes snuff.*) Your love is touching, but I can't reciprocate, that's all. (*Holding out the snuffbox to him.*) Help yourself.

MEDVEDENKO. Don't care for it. (*Pause.*)

MASHA. It's so muggy, there's bound to be a storm tonight. All you ever do is philosophize or talk about money. The way you think, there's nothing worse than being poor, but I think

---

8 He does not use the ordinary Russian word for indifference, *ravnodushie*, but the more exotic and pedantic *indifferentizm*.

it's a thousand times easier to wear rags and beg in the streets than . . . Oh well, you wouldn't understand.

SORIN and TREPLYOV enter right.

SORIN (*leaning on a stick*). My boy, this country life kind of has me all—you know—and take my word for it, I'll never get used to it. I went to bed last night at ten, and this morning I woke up feeling as if my brain were glued to my skull from too much sleep, and all the rest. (*Laughs.*) And after supper I accidentally fell asleep again, and now I'm a total wreck, I have nightmares, when's all said and done . . .

TREPLYOV. You're right, you ought to be living in town. (*On seeing Masha and Medvedenko.*) Friends, when it starts you'll be called, but you're not supposed to be here now. Please go away.

SORIN (*to Masha*). Mariya Ilyinishna, would you kindly ask your dad to untie the dog, the way it howls. My sister didn't get a wink of sleep again last night.

MASHA. Talk to my father yourself, because I won't. Leave me out of it, if you don't mind. (*To Medvedenko.*) Come on!

MEDVEDENKO. Be sure and let us know when it's about to start.

They both go out.

SORIN. Which means the dog'll howl all night again. It's the same old story. I never get my way in the country. Used to be you'd take a month's vacation and come here for relaxation and all the rest, but now they pester you with all sorts of rubbish, so one day of it and you're ready to make your escape. (*Laughs.*) I've always left this place with a sense of deep satisfaction . . . Well, but now I'm retired there's nowhere to escape to, when all's said and done. Like it or not, you stay . . .

YAKOV (*to Treplyov*). Konstantin Gavrilych, we're going for a swim.

TREPLYOV. All right, but be in your places in ten minutes. (*Looks at his watch.*) It'll be starting soon.

YAKOV. Yes, sir. (*Exits.*)

TREPLYOV (*looking over the platform*). This is what I call a theater. Curtain, downstage, upstage,[9] and beyond that empty space. No scenery at all. The view opens right on to the lake and the horizon. We'll take up the curtain at eight-thirty sharp, just when the moon's rising.

SORIN. Splendid.

TREPLYOV. If Miss Zarechnaya's late, of course, the whole effect will be spoiled. It's high time she got here. Her father and step-mother watch her like hawks, and it's as hard to pry her loose from that house as if it were a prison. (*He straightens his uncle's tie.*) Your hair and beard are a mess. You should get a haircut or something.

---

9 In the original, "First wing, then second," referring to the wing-and-border arrangement of the nineteenth-century stage. Treplyov is displaying his familiarity with theatrical jargon.

SORIN (*smoothing out his beard*). The tragedy of my life. Even when I was young I looked like I'd gone on a bender—and all the rest. Women never found me attractive. (*Sitting.*) How come my sister's in a bad mood?

TREPLYOV. How come? She's bored. (*Sitting beside him.*) She's jealous. She's already dead set against me and the performance and my play, because her novelist[10] might take a shine to Miss Zarechnaya.[11] She hasn't seen my play, but she hates it already . . .

SORIN (*laughs*). Can you imagine, honestly . . .

TREPLYOV. She's already annoyed that here on this little stage the success will belong to Miss Zarechnaya and not to her. (*After a glance at his watch.*) A case study for a psychology textbook—that's my mother. No argument she's talented, intelligent, ready to burst into tears over a novel, can rattle off reams of social protest poetry[12] by heart, has the bedside manner of an angel; but just try and praise a star like Duse[13]

---

10 Trigorin always uses the neutral, workmanlike word "writer" (*pisatel*) to describe himself, but Treplyov employs the more limited *belletrist*, a writer of fiction and light essays.

11 This line was excised by the censor. It was replaced by "because she isn't acting in it and Miss Zarechnaya is."

12 Literally, "can rattle off all of Nekrasov by heart"—Nikolay Alekseevich Nekrasov (1821–1878), Russian populist poet who called his inspiration the "Muse of vengeance and melancholy." His poems about the downtrodden masses, suffering peasants, and appeals for justice were popular parlor recitations at liberal gatherings in the 1880s, but Chekhov uses such recitations to indicate hypocrisy and posing in the reciter.

13 Eleonora Duse (1859–1924), the great Italian actress, who first toured Russia in 1891, where Chekhov saw her as Cleopatra. He wrote, on March 17, 1891, "I don't

to her face. O ho ho! You mustn't praise anybody but her, you must write about her, rhapsodize, go into ecstasies over her brilliant acting in flashy vehicles like *Camille* or *Drugged by Life*,[14] but now that that kind of stimulant isn't available here in the country, she gets bored and spiteful, and we're all against her, it's all our fault. On top of that she's superstitious, scared of whistling in the dressing room or the number thirteen.[15] And she's a tightwad. She's got seventy thousand in a bank in Odessa—I know it for a fact. But ask her for a loan and she'll go into hysterics.

SORIN. You've got it in your head that your mother doesn't like your play, so you're upset and all the rest. Take it easy, your mother adores you.

---

understand Italian, but she acted so well that I seemed to understand every word. Remarkable actress. I've never seen anything like her." Like George Bernard Shaw, he preferred her to her rival Sarah Bernhardt.

14 Arkadina's repertory consists of rather sensational, fashionably risqué dramas. *Camille* is *La Dame aux camélias* (1852), a play by Alexandre Dumas *fils*, concerning a courtesan with a heart of gold and lungs of tissue paper who gives up her love and eventually her life to advance her lover. It was first played in Russia in 1867, and later seen there during tours of Sarah Bernhardt in 1881 and 1892 and Eleonora Duse in 1892. Chekhov loathed *Drugged by Life*, a play by Boleslav Markevich, based on his novel *The Abyss*, and performed in Moscow in 1884 under the title *Olga Rantseva*. To quote Chekhov's review, "In general the play is written with a lavatory brush and stinks of obscenity." Its central character is a woman of loose morals, who, after four acts of dissipation and costume changes, dies in the fifth in an odor of sanctity. The connection to Arkadina's life and her expensive wardrobe is clear.

15 Literally, three candles on a table. This is a fatal omen, for at a Russian wake two candles were placed at the corpse's head, one at its feet. Therefore, if three lights are burning, one must be snuffed out.

TREPLYOV (*picking the petals from a flower*). She loves me—
she loves me not, she loves me—she loves me not, she loves
me—she loves me not. (*Laughs.*) You see, my mother doesn't
love me. Why should she! She wants to live, love, wear bright
colors, but I'm twenty-five, and a constant reminder that she's
not young anymore. When I'm not around, she's only thirty-
two; when I am, she's forty-three, and that's why she hates me.
She also knows that I don't believe in the theater. She loves the
theater, she thinks she's serving humanity, the sacred cause of
art, but as far as I'm concerned, the modern theater is trite, rid-
dled with clichés. When the curtain goes up on an artificially
lighted room with three walls, and these great talents, acolytes
of the religion of art, act out how people eat, drink, make love,
walk, wear their jackets; when they take cheap, vulgar plots and
cheap, vulgar speeches and try to extract a moral—not too big a
moral, easy on the digestion, useful around the house; when in
a thousand different ways they serve up the same old leftovers,
again and again and again—I run out the exit and keep on running, the way Maupassant ran from the Eiffel Tower,[16] because
it was crushing his brain beneath *its* tawdry vulgarity.

SORIN. You've got to have theater.

---

16 Guy de Maupassant (1850–1893), French writer, whose works began to appear
in Russian in 1894 and 1896. He died of syphilis and drugs, not modern technology.
The Eiffel Tower was erected by Gustave Eiffel in 1889 for the Paris Exposition and,
at 300 meters, was the highest man-made structure of the time. It was controversial,
many persons of taste considering it an eyesore. Maupassant detested it as a symbol of
materialism and modern vulgarity; he chose to dine at its restaurant, the only place in
Paris from which one could not see the tower.

TREPLYOV. New forms are what we need. New forms are what we need, and if there aren't any, then we're better off with nothing. (*Looks at his watch.*) I love my mother, love her deeply; but she smokes, drinks, lives openly with that novelist,[17] her name constantly in the papers—it gets me down. Sometimes it's just my plain human ego talking; it's a shame my mother is a famous actress, because I think if she were an ordinary woman, I might be happier. Uncle, can there be a more maddening and ridiculous situation than the one I'm in: her parties will be packed with celebrities, actors and writers, and I'll be the only nobody in the room, and they put up with me just because I'm her son. Who am I? What am I? Expelled from the University in my junior year for circumstances which, as they say, were beyond the editor's control,[18] with no talent at all, and no money either, according to my passport I'm a bourgeois from Kiev.[19] My father actually is a bourgeois from Kiev, but he was also a famous actor. So when all those actors and writers at her parties used to condescend with their kind attentions, I'd feel as if their eyes were sizing up how insignificant I was—I could guess what they were thinking and I'd go through agonies of humiliation.

17 This last phrase was excised by the censor, and replaced by Chekhov with "but she leads a disorderly life, constantly carrying on with that novelist."

18 A journalistic euphemism to cover passages deleted by the censorship. It suggests that Treplyov was expelled for political activity.

19 Literally, a Kievan *meshchanin*, that is, a burgher, townsman, artisan, or small tradesman. The word bears connotations of narrow-mindedness, philistinism, and parochialism. By marrying Treplyov's father, Arkadina had come down in station. And although Kiev, the capital of Ukraine, was the seventh most populous city in Russia, to be associated with it suggests provincialism.

SORIN. While we're on the subject, tell me, please, what sort of fellow is this novelist? I can't figure him out. He never opens his mouth.[20]

TREPLYOV. Clever enough, easygoing, a bit, what's the word, taciturn. He's all right. He's not even forty, but he's jaded, jaded within an inch of his life . . . Now he only drinks beer and can love only those who are no longer young . . .[21] As for his writing, it's . . . how can I put it? Charming, talented . . . but . . . compared to Tolstoy or Zola,[22] a little Trigorin goes a long way.

SORIN. But I love authors, my boy. There was a time when I desperately wanted two things: I wanted to get married and I wanted to be an author, but I didn't manage to do either one. Yes. It would be nice to be even a second-rate author, when all's said and done . . .

TREPLYOV (*listening hard*). I hear footsteps . . . (*Embraces his uncle.*) I can't live without her . . . Even the sound of her footsteps is musical . . . I'm out of my mind with happiness. (*Quickly goes to meet NINA ZARECHNAYA as she enters.*) Enchantress, girl of my dreams . . .

---

20 Nemirovich-Danchenko believed the character of Trigorin to be based on Chekhov's friend Ivan Potapenko, a successful novelist noted for his modesty, self-deprecation, lavish living, and appeal to women.

21 This phrase was excised by the censor and replaced by Chekhov with "already famous and jaded within an inch of his life . . ."

22 Lev Nikolaevich Tolstoy (1828–1910) was widely considered Russia's greatest author and her moral conscience. The works of Émile Zola (1840–1902) usually appeared in Russian translation shortly after their appearance in French.

NINA (*excited*). I'm not late . . . I'm sure I'm not late . . .

TREPLYOV (*kissing her hands*). No, no, no . . .

NINA. All day I've been on edge, I've been so worried! I was afraid Father wouldn't let me go . . . But he's just gone out with my stepmother. The sky was red, the moon's already on the rise, so I took a whip to the horses, lashed them. (*Laughs.*) But I'm glad I did. (*Squeezes Sorin's hand tightly.*)

SORIN (*laughs*). I do believe your pretty eyes have tears in them . . . Heh-heh! Mustn't do that!

NINA. You're right . . . You see the way I'm panting. In half an hour I've got to go, we must hurry. Don't, don't, for heaven's sake, don't make me late. Father doesn't know I'm here.

TREPLYOV. As a matter of fact, it is time to begin. I have to collect everybody.

SORIN. I'll go fetch 'em and all the rest. Right this minute. (*Crosses right and sings.*) "Back to France two grenadiers . . ."[23] (*Looking round.*) Once I started singing just like that, and some

---

23 The opening lines of a poem by Heinrich Heine, "Die beide Grenadiere" (1822), set to music by Robert Schumann (1827). The rest of the verse goes in translation:

> They had been imprisoned in Russia.
> And when they got to a German billet,
> They hung their heads.

According to Arthur Ganz, it is ironic that "one of the great romantic evocations of the power of the will (here a will that vows to seize upon its object even from beyond the grave), [is] precisely the quality that Sorin lacks" (*Drama Survey*, Spring 1966).

assistant D.A.[24] says to me, "Your Honor, that's a powerful voice you've got . . ." Then he thought a bit and added, "Powerful . . . but repulsive." (*Laughs and exits.*)

NINA. Father and his wife won't let me come here. They say this place is bohemian . . . they're afraid I might become an actress . . . But I'm drawn here to the lake, like a gull . . . My heart is filled with all of you. (*Looks around.*)

TREPLYOV. We're alone.

NINA. I think there's someone over there.

TREPLYOV. No one. (*They kiss.*)

NINA. What kind of tree is that?

TREPLYOV. Elm.

NINA. How come it's so dark?

TREPLYOV. It's nightfall, things get dark. Don't leave so soon, for my sake.

NINA. Can't.

TREPLYOV. What if I ride over to your place, Nina? I'll stand all night in the garden and stare at your window.

---

24 We learn later that Sorin had been an Actual State Councillor, fourth class in the tsarist table of ranks, equivalent to a Major-General and a Rear Admiral, so he is being twitted by an underling. A person who attains this rank may be addressed as "Your Excellency."

NINA. Can't, the watchman will catch you. Trésor still isn't used to you and he'll start barking.

TREPLYOV. I love you.

NINA. Ssh . . .

TREPLYOV (*having heard footsteps*). Who's there? That you, Yakov?

YAKOV (*behind the platform*). Right.

TREPLYOV. Got the methylated spirits? And the sulphur? When the red eyes make their entrance, there has to be a smell of sulphur. (*To Nina.*) Go on, they've got it all ready for you. Are you excited?

NINA. Yes, very. Your Mama doesn't count. I'm not afraid of her, but then there's Trigorin . . . Acting with him in the audience frightens and embarrasses me . . . A famous writer . . . Is he young?

TREPLYOV. Yes.

NINA. His stories are so wonderful!

TREPLYOV (*coldly*). I wouldn't know, I haven't read them.

NINA. It isn't easy to act in your play. There are no living characters in it.

TREPLYOV. Living characters! Life should be portrayed not the way it is, and not the way it's supposed to be, but the way it appears in dreams.

NINA. There isn't much action in your play, it's like a read-through.[25] And a play, I think, definitely ought to have love interest . . .

They both go behind the platform. Enter POLINA ANDREEVNA and DORN.

POLINA ANDREEVNA. It's starting to get damp. Go back, put on your galoshes.

DORN. I'm overheated.

POLINA ANDREEVNA. You don't take care of yourself. It's sheer obstinacy. You're a doctor and you know perfectly well that damp air is bad for you, but you want me to suffer; you deliberately sat up all last night on the veranda . . .

DORN (*sings*). "Say not that thy youth was wasted."[26]

POLINA ANDREEVNA. You were so infatuated talking to Irina Nikolaevna . . . you didn't notice the cold. Admit you're attracted to her.

DORN. I'm fifty-five years old.

POLINA ANDREEVNA. Don't be silly, that's not old for a man. You're beautifully preserved and women still find you attractive.

DORN. Then what can I do for you?

---

25 *Chitka*, which is theatrical slang. Nina's vocabulary has profited by listening to Arkadina.

26 A line from Nekrasov's poem "A heavy cross fell to her lot" (1856), set to music by Adolf Prigozhy.

POLINA ANDREEVNA. You're all of you ready to fall on your faces at an actress's feet. All of you!

DORN (*sings*). "Once again I stand before thee . . ."[27] If society loves actors and treats them differently from, say, shopkeepers, it's only natural. It's what's we call idealism.

POLINA ANDREEVNA. Women have always fallen in love with you and flung themselves at you. Do you call that idealism?

DORN (*shrugging*). So what? My relationships with women have always been a good thing. What they really loved was my being a first-class doctor. Ten or fifteen years ago, remember, I was the only competent obstetrician[28] in the whole county. Not to mention, I was a man of honor.

POLINA ANDREEVNA (*seizes him by the hand*). My dearest!

DORN. Hush. They're coming.

Enter ARKADINA, *arm in arm with* SORIN;
TRIGORIN, SHAMRAEV, MEDVEDENKO,
and MASHA.

SHAMRAEV. At the Poltava fair[29] in 1873 she gave a marvelous performance. Sheer delight! Wonderful acting! Would you

---

27 In full, "stand bewitched before thee," a line from V. I. Krasov's *Stanzas* (1842), set to music by Aleksandr Alyabiev.

28 Dorn uses the French word *accoucheur*, an indication of his refinement.

29 Capital of the *guberniya* of the same name, located in the Ukraine; its main industry was horse trading, slaughterhouses, and machinery manufacture. Its population was largely Little Russians (the standard tsarist term for Ukrainians) and Jews. Acting companies proliferated in such towns during the fairs.

also happen to know what's become of the comedian Chadin, Pavel Chadin? He was inimitable in *Krechinsky's Wedding*,[30] better than the great Sadovsky,[31] take my word for it, dear lady. Where is he these days?

ARKADINA. You're always asking me about these prehistoric characters. How should I know? (*Sits down.*)

SHAMRAEV (*sighs*). Good old Chadin! You don't see his like nowadays. The stage is going downhill, Irina Nikolaevna! In the old days there were mighty oaks, but now all you see are stumps.

DORN. There's not a lot of brilliant talent around these days, it's true, but the general level of acting has improved considerably.

SHAMRAEV. I can't agree with you there. Still, it's a matter of taste. *De gustibus, pluribus unum.*[32]

TREPLYOV *enters from behind the platform.*

ARKADINA (*to her son*). My darling son, when are we to begin?

---

30 In the original, "as Raspluev." "Ivan Antonovich, a small but thickset man around fifty," a great comic role in Aleksandr Sukhovo-Kobylin's *Krechinsky's Wedding* (first staged 1855), the cynical henchman of the confidence-man hero.

31 Stage name of Prov Mikhailovich Yermilov (1818–1872), a famous character actor and member of the Maly Theatre troupe in Moscow from 1839 to his death. He was responsible for the growing popularity of Ostrovsky's plays. Sukhovo-Kobylin believed that Sadovsky had vulgarized the part of Raspluev, which he created.

32 In the original, *de gustibus aut bene aut nihil*, a violent yoking together of three different Latin sayings: *De gustibus non disputantur*, "there's no point arguing over taste"; *De mortuis nil nisi bene*, "Say naught but good of the dead"; and *Aut Caesar aut nihil*, "Either Caesar or nothing."

TREPLYOV. In a minute. Have some patience.

ARKADINA (*reciting from* Hamlet).[33] "My son, Thou turn'st mine eyes into my very soul, And there I see such black and grainéd spots As will not leave their tinct."

TREPLYOV (*reciting from* Hamlet). "Then wherefore dost thou yield to sin, seeking love in a morass of crime?" (*A bugle is blown behind the platform.*) Ladies and gentlemen, we're about to begin! Your attention, please! (*Pause.*) I'm starting. (*Thumps with a stick and speaks loudly.*) O ye venerable and ancient shades, that nocturnally hover above this lake, put us to sleep and let us dream of what will be in two hundred thousand years!

SORIN. In two hundred thousand years, nothing will be.

TREPLYOV. Then let them reveal that nothing.

ARKADINA. Let them. We're asleep already.

> *The curtain rises; the vista onto the lake is revealed;*
> *the moon is over the horizon, reflected in the water;*
> *on a large boulder NINA ZARECHNAYA is seated,*
> *dressed all in white.*

NINA. Humans, lions, eagles and partridges, antlered deer, geese, spiders, silent fishes that inhabit the waters, starfish and those

---

33 A quotation from *Hamlet*, the closet scene, Act III, scene 3. In Nikolay Polevoy's Russian translation, Arkadina's quotation is reasonably accurate, but Treplyov's is a loose paraphrase of "making love over the nasty sty." The original image would have been too coarse for nineteenth-century playgoers and censors.

beings invisible to the naked eye,—in short, all living things, all living things, all living things, having completed the doleful cycle, are now extinct . . . Already thousands of centuries have passed since the earth bore any living creature, and this pale moon to no avail doth light her lamp. No more does the meadow awake to the cries of cranes, and the mayflies are no longer to be heard in the linden groves. Chilly, chilly, chilly. Empty, empty, empty. Ghastly, ghastly, ghastly. (*Pause.*) The bodies of living creatures have crumbled into dust, and Eternal Matter has converted them into stones, water, clouds, and all their souls are mingled into one. The universal soul—'tis I . . . in person . . . . In me are mingled the souls of Alexander the Great, and Caesar, and Shakespeare, and Napoleon, and the lowliest of leeches. In me human consciousness is mingled with animal instinct, and I remember everything, everything, everything, and I relive each life within myself.

Will-o'-the-wisps appear.

ARKADINA (*in a low voice*). This is something avant-garde.[34]

TREPLYOV (*entreating her reproachfully*). Mama!

NINA. I am alone. Once every hundred years I ope my lips to speak, and my voice echoes dolefully in this void, and no one hears . . . Even ye, pale fires, hear me not . . . Toward morning ye are engendered by the putrescence of the swamp, and

---

34 Literally, *chto-to dekadentskoe*, something decadent. At this time, symbolist and decadent writing, popularized by Maeterlinck, was considered the cutting edge of literary innovation in Europe, and was beginning to gain disciples in Russia.

roam till dawn, but sans thoughts, sans will, sans throbbing life. Fearing lest life spring up in you, the father of Eternal Matter, Satan, at every moment effects in you, as in stones and water, an interchange of atoms, and you transmutate incessantly. Throughout the universe there remains constant and immutable naught but spirit. (*Pause.*) Like a prisoner, flung into a deep empty pit, I know not where I am nor what awaits me. All that is revealed to me is that in the dogged, cruel struggle with Satan, the principle of material forces, it is decreed that I shall conquer, and thereafter matter and spirit shall blend in glorious harmony and the kingdom of universal will shall emerge. But this will come to pass only very gradually, over a long, long series of millennia, when the moon and the twinkling dog-star and the earth are turned to dust . . . But until that time, all will be ghastly, ghastly, ghastly . . . (*Pause; against the background of the lake two red dots appear.*) Behold, my mighty adversary, Satan, draws nigh. I see his dreadful crimson eyes . . .

ARKADINA. What a stink of sulphur. Is that necessary?

TREPLYOV. Yes.

ARKADINA (*laughs*). Of course, special effects.

TREPLYOV. Mama!

NINA. He misses human beings . . .

POLINA ANDREEVNA (*to Dorn*). You took off your hat. Put it back on, or you'll catch cold.

ARKADINA. The doctor's tipping his hat to Satan, the father of eternal matter.

TREPLYOV (*flaring up, loudly*). The play's over! That's enough! Curtain!

ARKADINA. What are you angry about?

TREPLYOV. Enough! Curtain! Ring down the curtain! (*Stamping his feet.*) Curtain! (*The curtain comes down.*) I apologize! I lost sight of the fact that playwriting and playacting are only for the chosen few. I infringed the monopoly! I feel . . . I . . . (*He wants to say something more, but waves his hand dismissively and exits left.*)

ARKADINA. What's come over him?

SORIN. Irina, dear heart, you mustn't treat a young man's self-esteem that way.

ARKADINA. What did I say to him?

SORIN. You offended him.

ARKADINA. He told us beforehand that it was a joke, so I treated his play as a joke.

SORIN. Even so . . .

ARKADINA. Now it turns out that he wrote a masterpiece! Pardon me for living! The real reason he staged this production and asphyxiated us with sulphur was not to make a joke, but to give us an object-lesson . . . He wanted to teach us how to write and how to act. This is starting to get tiresome. These constant jabs at me and digs, I don't care what you say, would get on anybody's nerves! Temperamental, conceited little boy.

SORIN. He wanted to give you a treat.

ARKADINA. Really? And yet you'll notice that he didn't pick an ordinary sort of play, but forced us to listen to this avant-garde gibberish. For the sake of a joke I'm willing to listen to gibberish too, but this is all pretentiousness about new forms, a new age in art. So far as I can tell, there's no new forms in it, nothing but a nasty disposition . . .

TRIGORIN. Everyone writes the way he wants and the way he can.

ARKADINA. Let him write the way he wants and the way he can, only let him leave me in peace.

DORN. "Mighty Jove, once angry grown . . ."[35]

ARKADINA. I'm not Jove, I'm a woman. (*Lighting a cigarette.*) I'm not angry, I'm only annoyed that a young man should waste his time in such a tiresome way. I didn't mean to offend him.

MEDVEDENKO. There's no basis for distinguishing spirit from matter, because spirit itself is probably an agglomeration of material atoms. (*Eagerly, to Trigorin.*) Now, you know, somebody ought to write a play and get it produced about—our friend the schoolteacher. He leads a tough, tough life!

---

35 A saying that continues "has stopped being Jove" or "is in the wrong."

ARKADINA. That's all very true, but don't let's talk about plays or atoms. What a glorious night! Do you hear the singing, ladies and gentlemen?[36] (*Listening hard.*) How lovely!

POLINA ANDREEVNA. It's on the other side of the lake.

Pause.

ARKADINA (*to Trigorin*). Sit beside me. Some ten or fifteen years ago, here, on the lake, you could hear music and singing nonstop almost every night. There were six country houses along the shore. I can remember laughter, noise-making, shooting, and one love affair after another . . . The romantic lead and idol of all six houses at that time is among us, may I present (*nods to Dorn*) Doctor Yevgeny Dorn. He's fascinating even now, but in those days he was irresistible. However, my conscience is starting to bother me. Why did I insult my poor little boy? I feel bad about it. (*Loudly.*) Kostya! My child! Kostya!

MASHA. I'll go look for him.

ARKADINA. Please do, darling.

MASHA (*crosses left*). Yoo-hoo! Konstantin! . . . Yoo-hoo! (*Exits.*)

NINA (*coming out from behind the platform*). It looks like we're not going to go on, so I can come out. Good evening! (*Exchanges kisses with Arkadina and Polina Andreevna.*)

---

36 The Moscow Art Theatre used Glinka's *Temptation*.

SORIN. Bravo! Bravo!

ARKADINA. Bravo, bravo! We loved it. With such looks, such a wonderful voice it's wrong, it's criminal to vegetate in the country. You probably have talent too. You hear me? You have an obligation to go on the stage!

NINA. Oh, that's my fondest dream! (*Sighs.*) But it will never come true.

ARKADINA. Who knows? May I introduce: Boris Trigorin.

NINA. Ah, I'm delighted . . . (*Embarrassed.*) I read all your things . . .

ARKADINA (*seating her beside her*). Don't be embarrassed, darling. He's a celebrity, but he's a simple soul. You see, he's embarrassed himself.

DORN. I suppose we can raise the curtain now, it feels spooky this way.

SHAMRAEV (*loudly*). Yakov, haul up that curtain, boy!

The curtain is raised.

NINA (*to Trigorin*). It's a strange play, isn't it?

TRIGORIN. I didn't understand a word. Still, I enjoyed watching it. Your acting was so sincere. And the scenery was gorgeous. (*Pause.*) I suppose there are a lot of fish in that lake.

NINA. Yes.

TRIGORIN. I love fishing. For me there's no greater pleasure than sitting on the bank at dusk, watching the float bob up and down.[37]

NINA. But, I should think, anyone who's enjoyed creating a work of art couldn't enjoy anything else.

ARKADINA (*laughing*). Don't talk like that. Whenever anyone compliments him, he just shrivels up.

SHAMRAEV. I remember at the Moscow Opera House once the famous Silva[38] hit low C. And at the time, as luck would have it, sitting in the gallery was the bass from our church choir, and all of a sudden, you can imagine our intense surprise, we hear from the gallery: "Bravo, Silva!"—a whole octave lower . . . Something like this (*in a basso profundo*): Bravo, Silva . . . The audience was dumbfounded.

Pause.

DORN. The quiet angel just flew by.[39]

NINA. My time's up. Good-bye.

ARKADINA. Where are you off to? So early? We won't let you go.

---

37 Chekhov's two favorite pastimes in the country were fishing with a float—a cork attached to a weighted line that moves when a fish bites—and gathering mushrooms.

38 Although Éloi Silva, a Belgian tenor born in 1846, was a star at the Petersburg Italian opera, mainly in Meyerbeer, Chekhov has simply lifted the name and applied it to a bass.

39 A common saying, used whenever a pause suddenly falls over a conversation. Chekhov uses it in his stories frequently.

NINA. Papa's waiting for me.

ARKADINA. That man, honestly . . . (*Exchanges kisses.*) Well, what can we do. It's a shame, a crying shame to let you go.

NINA. If you only knew how hard it is for me to leave!

ARKADINA. Somebody should see you home, you darling girl.

NINA (*alarmed*). Oh, no, no!

SORIN (*to her, imploring*). Do stay!

NINA. I can't, Pyotr Nikolaevich.

SORIN. Do stay just one more hour and all the rest. Now, how 'bout it, come on . . .

NINA (*after thinking it over, tearfully*). I can't! (*Shakes hands and exits hurriedly.*)

ARKADINA. The girl's really and truly unhappy. They say her late mother bequeathed her husband her whole huge fortune, down to the last penny, and now this child is left with nothing, because her father's already willed it to his second wife. It's outrageous.

DORN. Yes, her dear old dad is a pedigreed swine. Credit where credit's due.

SORIN (*rubbing his chilled hands*). We'd best be going too, ladies and gentlemen, it's starting to get damp. My legs ache.

ARKADINA. They must be wooden legs, they can hardly move. Well, let's go, you star-crossed old man. (*Takes him by the arm.*)

SHAMRAEV (*offering his arm to his wife*). Madame?

SORIN. I hear that dog howling again. (*To Shamraev.*) Kindly see that he's unchained, Ilya Afanasevich.

SHAMRAEV. Can't be done, Pyotr Nikolaevich, I'm afraid robbers might break into the barn. Got my millet stored there. (*To Medvedenko, walking beside him.*) Yes, a whole octave lower: "Bravo, Silva!" Wasn't a professional singer, either, just an ordinary member of the church choir.

MEDVEDENKO. How much does an ordinary member of the church choir make?

They all go out, except DORN.

DORN (*alone*). I don't know, maybe I'm confused or I'm crazy but I liked the play. There's something in it. When that girl was talking about being lonely and then, when Satan's red eyes appeared, my hands trembled with excitement. Fresh, naive . . . Oh, I think he's coming this way. I'd like to tell him the nicest things I can.

TREPLYOV (*enters*). Nobody's here.

DORN. I am.

TREPLYOV. That Masha creature's been looking for me all over the park. Unbearable female.

DORN. Konstantin Gavrilovich, I liked your play very much. It's an unusual piece of work, and I didn't get to hear how it ends, but even so, it makes a powerful impression. You're a talented fellow, you ought to keep at it. (*TREPLYOV squeezes his hand tightly and embraces him impulsively.*) Foo, don't be so high-strung. Tears in his eyes . . . What was I saying? You took a subject from the realm of abstract ideas. That was appropriate, because a work of art definitely ought to express a great idea. The beauty of a thing lies entirely in its seriousness. You're awfully pale!

TREPLYOV. Then what you're saying is—keep at it!

DORN. Yes . . . But write about only what's important and everlasting. You know, I've lived my life with variety and discrimination; I've had it all, but if I ever got the chance to experience the spiritual uplift artists feel at the moment of creation, I think I'd relinquish my physical trappings and all that they entail, and let myself be wafted far away from earth into the empyrean.

TREPLYOV. Sorry, where's Miss Zarechnaya?

DORN. And another thing. Every work of art ought to have a clear, well-defined idea. You ought to know what you're writing for, otherwise if you travel this picturesque path without a well-defined goal, you'll go astray and your talent will destroy you.

TREPLYOV (*impatiently*). Where's Miss Zarechnaya?

DORN. She went home.

TREPLYOV (*in despair*). What am I going to do? I have to see her . . . I 've got to see her . . . I'm going . . .

MASHA *enters.*

DORN (*to Treplyov*). Calm down, my friend.

TREPLYOV. But I'm going anyway. I have to go.

MASHA. Come home, Konstantin Gavrilovich. Your Mama's waiting for you. She's worried.

TREPLYOV. Tell her I've gone. And will you all please leave me in peace! Stay here! Don't come after me!

DORN. Now, now, now, my dear boy . . . you musn't act this way . . . isn't nice.

TREPLYOV (*tearfully*). Good-bye, Doctor. Thanks . . . (*Exits.*)

DORN (*sighs*). Youth, youth!

MASHA. When people have nothing better to say, they go: youth, youth . . . (*Takes snuff.*)

DORN (*takes away her snuffbox and tosses it into the bushes*). That's disgusting! (*Pause.*) Sounds like music in the house. Better go in.

MASHA. Wait.

DORN. What?

MASHA. I want to tell you something else. I have to talk to some-one . . . (*Getting excited.*) I don't love my father . . . but I feel close to you.[40] Why do I feel so intensely that we have some-

---

40 In an early draft of the play, Masha's father was revealed to be Dr. Dorn at this point. When the play was revived at the Moscow Art Theatre, Nemirovich-Danchenko advised Chekhov to eliminate this plot element:

> I said either this theme has to be developed or else entirely removed. Especially since it ends the first act. The end of a first act by its very nature has to wind up

thing in common . . . Help me. Help me, or I'll do something stupid, I'll mess up my life, wreck it . . . I can't stand it anymore . . .

DORN. What do you mean? Help you how?

MASHA. I'm in pain. Nobody, nobody knows how much pain I'm in. (*Lays her head on his chest, quietly.*) I love Konstantin.

DORN. They're all so high-strung! They're all so high-strung! And all this love . . . Oh, spellbinding lake! (*Tenderly.*) But what can I do, my child? What? What?

Curtain

ACT TWO

A croquet lawn. Up right, a house with a wide veranda, the lake can be seen, with the sun's rays reflected on it. Flowerbeds. Midday. Hot. To one side of the croquet lawn, in the shade of an old linden tree,

---

tightly the situation to be developed in the second act.

Chekhov said, "The audience does like it when at the end of an act a loaded gun is aimed at it."

"True enough," I replied, "but then it has to go off, and not simply be chucked away during the intermission."

It turns out that later on Chekhov repeated this remark more than a few times.

He agreed with me. The ending was revised.

(Vl. I. Nemirovich-Danchenko, *Out of the Past* [1938])

ARKADINA, DORN, and MASHA are sitting on a
bench. DORN has an open book on his lap.

ARKADINA (*to Masha*). Come on, let's get up. (*Both rise.*) Let's stand side by side. You're twenty-two, and I'm nearly twice that. Yevgeny Sergeich, which of us is younger?[41]

DORN. You, of course.

ARKADINA. Thank you, kind sir . . . And why? Because I work, I feel emotions, I'm constantly on the go, while you sit still in the same place; you don't live . . . And I have a rule: don't peer into the future. I never give a thought to old age or death. What will be will be.

MASHA. But I feel as if I were born ages and ages ago; I lug my life around like a dead weight, like the endless train on a gown . . . And lots of times I don't feel much like going on living. (*Sits.*) Of course, this is all silly. I have to shake myself out of it, slough it off.

DORN (*sings quietly*). "Tell her of love, flowers of mine . . ."[42]

---

41 In Chekhov's story "Ariadne" (1895) there is a similar passage:

"I just wonder, sir, how you can live without love?" he said. "You are young, handsome, interesting,—in short, you are a fashion plate of a man, but you live like a monk. Ah, these old men of twenty-eight! I am almost ten years older than you, but which of us is the younger? Ariadne Grigoryevna, who is younger?"
"You, of course," replied Ariadne.

42 Siébel's song in Act III, scene one, of Gounod's opera *Faust*. In Russia, quoting it meant "You're talking through your hat."

ARKADINA. Besides, I'm as neat and tidy as an English gentle-
man. Darling, I keep myself up to the mark, if I say so myself,
and I'm always dressed and have my hair done *comme il faut*.[43]
Would I ever venture to leave the house, just step into the garden, in a smock or with my hair down? Never. The reason I'm
in such good shape is because I was never sloppy, never let
myself go, like some people . . . (*With her hands on her hips,
strides up and down the lawn.*) There you see — light on my feet.
Fit to play a girl of fifteen.

DORN. Fine and dandy, but regardless of all that I'll go on reading. (*Picks up the book.*) We'd stopped at the grain merchant
and the rats.

ARKADINA. And the rats. Read away. (*Sits down.*) Actually, give
it to me, I'll read it. 'S my turn. (*Takes the book and runs her
eyes over it.*) And the rats . . . Here we go . . . (*Reads.*) "And, of
course, for people in society to pamper novelists and lure them
into their homes is as dangerous as if a grain merchant were to
breed rats in his granaries. Meanwhile they go on loving them.
So, when a woman has picked out the writer she wishes to cap-
tivate, she lays siege to him by means of compliments, endear-
ments and flattering attentions . . . "[44] Well, that may be what

---

43 French, "properly, suitably."

44 From *Sur l'eau* (1888), Maupassant's diary of a Mediterranean cruise, taken to
restore his shattered nerves. The passage continues:

Just like water, which, drop by drop, pierces the hardest rock, praise falls, word
by word, on the sensitive heart of a man of letters. So, as soon as she sees
he is tenderized, moved, won over by this constant flattery, she isolates him,
she gradually cuts the connections he might have elsewhere, and insensibly

the French do, but there's nothing of the sort in our country, we have no master plan. In Russia before a woman captivates a writer, she's usually fallen head over heels in love with him herself, take my word for it. You don't have far to look, just consider me and Trigorin.

Enter SORIN, leaning on a stick, next to NINA;
MEDVEDENKO wheels an empty armchair
behind them.

SORIN (*in the tone used to coddle children*). Are we? Are we having fun? Are we happy today, when's all said and done? (*To his sister.*) We're having fun! Father and Stepmother have gone out of town, and now we're free for three whole days.

NINA (*sits beside Arkadina and embraces her*). I'm happy! Now I can be all yours.

SORIN (*sits in the armchair*). She's the prettiest little thing today.

ARKADINA. Smartly dressed, interesting . . . You're clever at that sort of thing. (*Kisses Nina.*) But we mustn't praise her too much, or we'll put a hex on her.[45] Where's Boris Alekseevich?

NINA. He's down by the swimming hole, fishing.

---

accustoms him to come to her house, to enjoy himself there, to put his mind at ease there. To get him nicely acclimated to her house, she looks after him and prepares his success, puts him in the limelight, as a star, shows him, ahead of all the former habitués of the place, a marked consideration, an unequaled admiration.

45 Literally, "put the evil eye on her," presumably by arousing envy.

ARKADINA. I'm surprised he doesn't get fed up with it! (*About to go on reading.*)

NINA. What have you got there?

ARKADINA. "At Sea" by Maupassant, sweetheart. (*Reads a few lines to herself.*) Well, the rest is uninteresting and untrue. (*Closes the book.*) I feel uneasy. Tell me, what's the matter with my son? How come he's so tiresome and surly? He spends whole days on the lake, and I almost never see him.

MASHA. He's sick at heart. (*To Nina, shyly.*) Please, do recite something from his play!

NINA (*shrugs*). You want me to? It's so uninteresting!

MASHA (*with restrained excitement*). Whenever he recites, his eyes blaze and his face turns pale. He has a beautiful, mournful voice; and the look of a poet.

SORIN's snoring is audible.

DORN. Sweet dreams!

ARKADINA. Petrusha!

SORIN. Aah?

ARKADINA. You asleep?

SORIN. Certainly not.

Pause.

ARKADINA. You don't look after yourself, and you should, brother.

SORIN. I'd be glad to look after myself, but the doctor here won't prescribe a treatment.

DORN. Treatments at age sixty!

SORIN. Even at sixty a person wants to go on living.

DORN (*vexed*). Oh yeah! Well, take a couple of aspirins.[46]

ARKADINA. I think he'd feel better if he went to a health spa.

DORN. Think so? Let him go. Then again, let him stay here.

ARKADINA. Try and figure *that* out.

DORN. There's nothing to figure out. It's perfectly clear.

Pause.

MEDVEDENKO. The best thing Pyotr Nikolaevich could do is stop smoking.

SORIN. Rubbish.

DORN. No, it's not rubbish. Alcohol and tobacco rob you of your personality. After a cigar or a shot of vodka, you're not Pyotr Nikolaevich anymore, you're Pyotr Nikolaevich plus somebody else; your sense of self, your "ego" gets fuzzy around the edges, and you start talking about yourself in the third person — as "that other fellow."

---

46 Valerian, a mild sedative, the equivalent of aspirin (which was not widely marketed until 1899). The nervous actors of the Moscow Art Theatre, on the opening night of *The Seagull*, had dosed themselves heavily with valerian.

SORIN (*laughs*). 'S all right for you to lecture me! You've lived in your lifetime, but what about me? I worked in the Department of Justice for twenty-eight years, but I still haven't lived, haven't had any experiences, when all's said and done, and, take my word for it, I've still got a lust for life. You're jaded, you don't care, and so you can be philosophical, but I want to live a little and so I drink sherry at dinner and smoke cigars and all the rest. So there and all the rest.

DORN. A man should take life seriously, but trying treatments at sixty, complaining there wasn't enough fun in your youth is, pardon me, ridiculous.

MASHA (*rises*). Time for lunch, I guess . . . (*Walks with a sluggish, unsteady gait.*) Foot fell asleep . . . (*Exits.*)

DORN. She'll go and knock down a couple of drinks before lunch.

SORIN. The poor thing's got no happiness in her life.

DORN. Piffle, Your Excellency.

SORIN. You talk like a man who's had it all.

ARKADINA. Ah, what can be more boring than this darling rural boredom! Hot, quiet, nobody lifts a finger, everybody philosophizes . . . It's nice being with you, my friends, lovely listening to you, but . . . sitting in my hotel room and learning my lines—what could be better!

NINA (*rapturously*). How wonderful! I know just what you mean.

SORIN. Of course things're better in town. You sit in your office, the doorman doesn't let anyone in without being announced, the telephone . . . cabs on every corner and all the rest . . .

DORN (*sings*). "Tell her of love, flowers of mine . . ."

Enter SHAMRAEV, followed by POLINA ANDREEVNA.

SHAMRAEV. Here's our crowd. Good morning! (*Kisses Arkadina's hand, then Nina's.*) The wife tells me you're planning to drive with her into town today. Is that right?

ARKADINA. Yes, that's our plan.

SHAMRAEV. Hm . . . That's just great, but how you do expect to get there, dear lady? Our rye is being carted today, all the hired hands are busy. And which horses will you take, may I ask?

ARKADINA. Which? How should I know which?

SORIN. We've still got the carriage horses.

SHAMRAEV (*getting excited*). Carriage horses? And where am I to get harnesses? Where am I to get harnesses? This is marvelous! This is incredible! Dear, dear lady! Forgive me, I bow down to your talent, I'm ready to give up ten years of my life for your sake, but horses I cannot give you.

ARKADINA. And what if I have to go? A fine how-do-you-do!

SHAMRAEV. Dear lady! You don't know what it means to run a farm!

ARKADINA (*flaring up*). Here we go again! In that case, I shall leave for Moscow this very day. Have them hire horses for me in town, or else I'll go to the station on foot!

SHAMRAEV (*flaring up*). In that case I tender my resignation! Go find yourself another overseer. (*Exits.*)

ARKADINA. Every summer it's the same thing, every summer I'm exposed to insults. I'll never set foot in this place again! (*Exits left, where the swimming hole is supposed to be; in a minute she can be seen crossing into the house; TRIGORIN follows her with fishing poles*[47] *and a pail.*)

SORIN (*flaring up*). This is a disgrace! This is who the hell knows what! This is going to make me lose my temper, when all's said and done. Bring all the horses here this very minute!

NINA (*to Polina Andreevna*). To refuse Irina Nikolaevna, a famous actress! Isn't every one of her wishes, even her whims, more important than your farming? It's just incredible!

POLINA ANDREEVNA (*in despair*). What can I do? Put yourself in my position: what can I do?

---

47 "I was rehearsing Trigorin in *The Seagull*. And Anton Pavlovich invited me himself to talk over the role. I arrived with trepidation.

"'You know,' Anton Pavlovich began, 'the fishing poles ought to be, you know, homemade, bent. He makes them himself with a penknife . . . The cigar is a good one . . . Maybe it's not a really good one, but it definitely has to have silver paper . . .'

"Then he fell silent, thought a bit and said:

"'But the main thing is the fishing-poles . . .'" (Vasily Kachalov, *Shipovnik Almanac* 23 [1914]).

Chekhov shared Trigorin's love of fishing and wrote in a letter, "To catch a perch! It's finer and sweeter than love!"

SORIN (*to Nina*). Let's go in to my sister . . . We'll all plead with her not to leave. Isn't that the thing? (*Looking in the direction of Shamraev's exit.*) Insufferable fellow! Dictator!

NINA (*helping him to rise*). Sit down, sit down . . . We'll wheel you . . . (*She and MEDVEDENKO wheel the armchair.*) Oh, this is just awful!

SORIN. Yes, yes, this is awful . . . But he won't leave, I'll talk it over with him.

> *They leave; only DORN and POLINA*
> *ANDREEVNA remain.*

DORN. People are so predictable. Ultimately the right thing would simply be to toss your husband out on his ear, but in fact it'll end up with that old fusspot Pyotr Nikolaevich and his sister begging *him* for forgiveness. Wait and see!

POLINA ANDREEVNA. He even sent the carriage horses into the fields. And every day there are squabbles like that. If you only knew how it upsets me! It's making me ill: you see, I'm trembling . . . I can't put up with his crudeness. (*Beseeching.*) Yevgeny, dearest, light of my life, take me with you . . . Time's running out for us, we aren't young anymore, now at least when our lives are over, let's stop hiding, stop lying . . . (*Pause.*)

DORN. I'm fifty-five years old, it's too late for me to change my way of life.

POLINA ANDREEVNA. I know, you're rejecting me because there are other women you're intimate with too. You can't possibly take all of them in. I understand. Forgive me, I'm getting on your nerves.

NINA appears near the house; she is plucking flowers.

DORN. No, not at all.

POLINA ANDREEVNA. I'm sick with jealousy. Of course, you're a doctor, there's no way you can avoid women. I understand . . .

DORN (*to Nina, who walks by*). How are things indoors?

NINA. Irina Nikolaevna's crying and Pyotr Nikolaevich is having an asthma attack.

DORN (*rises*). I'll go give them both some aspirin . . .

NINA (*offers him the flowers*). Please take these!

DORN. *Merci bien.* (*Goes into the house.*)

POLINA ANDREEVNA (*going with him*). What adorable little flowers! (*Near the house, in a muffled voice.*) Give me those flowers! Give me those flowers! (*Once she gets the flowers, she tears them up and throws them aside. They both go into the house.*)

NINA (*alone*). How odd to see a famous actress crying, and over such a trivial matter! And isn't it odd, a best-selling author, a favorite with the reading public, written up in all the papers, his portrait on sale, translated into foreign languages, yet he spends the whole day fishing and he's overjoyed when he catches a couple of perch. I thought that famous people were proud, inaccessible, that they despised the public and their own fame, their celebrity was a kind of revenge for blue blood and wealth being considered more respectable . . . But here they are crying, fishing, playing cards, laughing, and losing their tempers, like anybody else . . .

TREPLYOV (*enters bare-headed, carrying a rifle and a slain gull*). You're alone here?

NINA. Alone. (*TREPLYOV lays the gull at her feet.*) What does this mean?

TREPLYOV. I did something nasty, I killed this gull today. I lay it at your feet.

NINA. What's wrong with you? (*Picks up the gull and stares at it.*)

TREPLYOV (*after a pause*). I'll soon kill myself the very same way.

NINA. I don't know who you are anymore.

TREPLYOV. Yes, ever since I stopped knowing who you are. You've changed toward me, your eyes are cold, my being here makes you tense.

NINA. Lately you've been so touchy, and you talk in code, symbols of some kind. And this gull is obviously a symbol too, but, forgive me, I don't understand it . . . (*Lays the gull on the bench.*) I'm too ordinary to understand you.

TREPLYOV. It started that night when my play was a stupid fiasco. Women don't forgive failure. I burned everything, everything to the last scrap of paper. If only you knew how unhappy I am! Your coolness to me is horrible, incredible, it's like waking up and seeing that the lake has suddenly dried up or sunk into the ground. You say you're too ordinary to understand me. Oh, what's there to understand? You didn't like my play, you despise my ideas, you've started thinking of me as a mediocrity, a nobody, like all the rest . . . (*Stamping his foot.*) That's something *I* understand, oh, I understand all right! There's a kind of spike stuck in my brain, damn it and damn my vanity, which sucks my blood, sucks it like a snake . . . (*Catching sight of TRIGORIN, who is walking and reading a notebook.*) There goes the real genius; he paces the ground like Hamlet, and with a book too. (*Mimicking.*) "Words, words, words . . ."[48] His sun hasn't even shone on you yet, but already you're smiling, your eyes are thawing in his rays. I won't stand in your way. (*He exits quickly.*)

TRIGORIN (*making notes in the book*). Takes snuff and drinks vodka . . . Always wears black. Courted by a schoolteacher . . .

NINA. Good afternoon, Boris Alekseevich!

TRIGORIN. Good afternoon. Circumstances have taken an unexpected turn, so it turns out we leave today. In all likelihood we'll never see one another again. And that's a pity. I don't often get the chance to meet young girls, young and interesting ones; I've long forgotten, I can't quite imagine what it must feel like to be eighteen, nineteen, and that's why in my novellas

---

48 *Polonius*: What do you read, my lord?
Hamlet: Words, words, words. (*Hamlet*, Act II, scene 2)

Treplyov's mention of the sun may reflect his unconscious recollection of Hamlet's earlier lines about Ophelia, that she not stand too much "i' the sun."

and stories the young girls are usually stilted. I really would like to be in your shoes, if just for an hour, to find out how your mind works and more or less what sort of stuff you're made of.

NINA. And I should like to be in your shoes.

TRIGORIN. What for?

NINA. To find out how it feels to be a famous, talented writer. How does fame feel? How do you realize that you're famous?

TRIGORIN. How? Nohow, I suppose. I never thought about it. (*Thinking it over.*) It's either-or: either you're exaggerating my fame or there's no real way to realize it.

NINA. But what about seeing your name in the papers?

TRIGORIN. If it's praise, I feel good, and if it's a scolding, then I'm in a bad mood for a couple of days.

NINA. The world's amazing! How I envy you, if you only knew! People's fates are so different. Some people can barely crawl through their boring, obscure existence, the same as everyone else, all unhappy; still others, like you, for instance—you're one in a million—are granted a life that's interesting, brilliant, meaningful . . . You're happy . . .

TRIGORIN. Am I? (*Shrugging.*) Hm . . . You stand here talking about fame, happiness, a brilliant, interesting life,[49] but to me

---

49 Compare Chekhov's letter to M. V. Kiselyova, September 21, 1886: ". . . It's no great treat to be a great writer. First, the life is gloomy . . . Work from morn to night, and not much profit . . . The money would make a cat weep . . ."

it sounds sweet and gooey, sorry, just like marshmallows, which I never eat. You're very young and very kind.

NINA. Your life is so beautiful!

TRIGORIN. What's so especially good about it? (*Looks at his watch.*) I ought to get some writing in now. Forgive me, I've got no time . . . (*Laughs.*) You've stepped on my pet corn, as the saying goes,[50] and now I'm starting to get upset and a little bit angry. All right, let me make a statement. Let's talk about my beautiful, brilliant life . . . Well, now, where shall we begin? (*After thinking a bit.*) Some people are obsessive compulsives, a person who thinks all the time, for instance, about the moon, well, I have my own particular moon. All the time, I'm obsessed with one compulsive thought: I have to write, I have to write, I have to . . . I've barely finished one story, when already for some reason I have to write another, then a third, after the third a fourth . . . I write nonstop, like an express train, and I can't help it. What's so beautiful and brilliant about that, I ask you? Oh, what an uncivilized way of life! I'm here talking to you, I'm getting excited, but meanwhile I never forget there's a story of mine waiting to be finished. I see that cloud over there, that looks like a grand piano. I think: have to refer to that somewhere in a story, a cloud drifted by that looked like a grand piano. I catch a whiff of heliotrope,[51]

---

50 An English comic phrase, from the works of the humorist Jerome K. Jerome, who was very popular in Russia.

51 *Heliotropium peruvianum*, a small blue or dark-blue flower, with a faint aroma of vanilla.

I instantly reel it in on my moustache: cloying smell, widow's color, refer to it in describing a summer evening. I'm angling in myself and you for every phrase, every word, and I rush to lock up all these words and phrases in my literary icebox: some time or other they'll come in handy! When I finish work, I run to the theater or go fishing; should be able to relax there, forget myself, oh, no, a heavy cannonball has started rolling around in my head—a new subject, and I'm drawn back to my desk, hurry, hurry, write, write. And so it goes forever and ever and ever, and I know no peace, and I feel that I'm devouring my own life, that to give away honey to somebody out there in space I'm robbing my finest flowers of their pollen, tearing up those flowers and trampling on their roots. Wouldn't you say I'm crazy? Surely my friends and relatives don't behave as if I were sane? "What are you puttering with now?"[52] What will you give us next?" The same old same old, and I start thinking that this friendly attention, praise, admiration—it's all a plot, they're humoring me like an invalid, and sometimes I'm afraid that they're just on the verge of creeping up behind me, grabbing me and clapping me into a straitjacket, like the madman in Gogol's story.[53] And years ago, the years of my youth, my best years, when I was starting out, my writing was sheer

---

52 Rather than the verb *pisat*, to write, Chekhov uses *popisyvat*, which, as George Calderon put it, "suggests that his writing is a sort of game, something that serves to keep him out of mischief. The critic Mikhailovsky used it, in the early days, of Chekhov's compositions."

53 Poprishchin, the hero of Gogol's "Diary of a Madman," a minor bureaucrat whose frantic scribbling reveals his delusions of adequacy. He falls in love with the daughter of his bureau chief and ends up in a madhouse.

agony. A second-rate writer, especially when luck isn't with him, sees himself as clumsy, awkward, irrelevant, his nerves are shot, frayed; he can't help hanging around people connected with literature and art, unrecognized, unnoticed by anyone, afraid to look them boldly in the face, like a compulsive gambler who's run out of money. I couldn't visualize my reader, but for that very reason he loomed in my imagination as hostile, suspicious. I was afraid of the public, it terrified me, and every time a new play of mine managed to get produced,[54] I thought the dark-haired spectators disliked it, while the fair-haired spectators couldn't care less. Oh, it's awful! Excruciating![55]

NINA. I'm sorry, but surely inspiration and the creative process itself must provide sublime moments of happiness?

TRIGORIN. Yes. When I'm writing, it's nice enough. And correcting the proofs is nice too, but . . . it's barely come off the presses, when I can't stand it, and can see that it's not right, a mistake, that it shouldn't have been written just that way, and I'm annoyed, feel rotten inside . . . (*Laughing.*) Then the public reads it: "Yes, charming, talented . . . Charming, but a far cry from Tolstoy," or "Lovely piece of work, but not up to Turgenev's *Fathers and Sons*."[56] And so until my dying day all I'll hear is charming and

---

54 This reflects Chekhov's own feelings after the opening of the revised *Ivanov* in 1889.

55 Tolstoy considered this speech the only good thing in the play. Chekhov himself considered obsessional writing to be the sign of a true writer.

56 The most famous novel (1862) of Ivan Sergeevich Turgenev (1818–1883), con-

talented, charming and talented—, and when I die, my friends will file past my grave and say, "Here lies Trigorin. He wasn't so bad as a writer, but no Turgenev."

NINA. Forgive me, I refuse to accept that. You're simply spoiled by success.

TRIGORIN. What do you call success? I'm never satisfied with myself, I don't like myself as a writer. Worst of all is when I'm in some sort of trance and often I don't even understand what I'm writing . . . I love the water over there, the trees, sky, I have a feeling for nature; it inspires me with a passion, the irresistible urge to write. But I'm really more than just a landscape painter;[57] I do have a social conscience as well, I love my country, the people. I feel that if I'm a writer, I have an obligation to discuss the people, their suffering, their future, discuss science, human rights, et cetera, et cetera, and I do discuss all of it, trip over myself; I'm attacked from every side, I make people angry, I hurtle back and forth like a fox hunted down by hounds. I see that life and science keep moving farther and farther ahead, while I keep falling farther and farther behind, like a peasant who's missed his train and, when all's said and done, I feel that all I know how to write about is landscapes, and everything else I write is phony, phony to the nth degree!

cerning a generational conflict, and offering a pattern of the "New Man." Chekhov gave the conflict between the generations a new twist in *The Seagull.*

57 Chekhov was the friend and admirer of the landscape painter Isaak Levitan, who tried to commit suicide in October 1895.

NINA. You've been working too hard, and you've got no time or desire to admit your own importance. Even if you're dissatisfied with yourself, other people think you're great and beautiful! If I were a writer, like you, I would devote my whole life to the public, but I'd realize that their only happiness lay in being brought up to my level, and they would be yoked to my chariot.

TRIGORIN. Well, well, a chariot . . . Am I Agamemnon or something?[58]

Both smile.

NINA. For the joy of being a writer or an actress, I would put up with my family disowning me, poverty, disappointment; I would live in a garret and eat nothing but black bread, suffer dissatisfaction with myself and realize my own imperfection, but in return I would insist on fame . . . real, resounding fame . . . (*Hides her face in her hands.*) My head's spinning . . . Oof!

ARKADINA's voice from the house: "Boris Alekseevich!"

TRIGORIN. They're calling me . . . I suppose it's about packing. But I don't feel like leaving. (*Looks around at the lake.*) Just look at this, God's country! . . . It's lovely!

NINA. You see the house and garden across the lake?

---

58 Agamemnon, leader of the Greek host in the Trojan war, was more familiar to Chekhov from Offenbach's comic opera *La Belle Hélène* (1864) than from Homer's *Iliad*.

TRIGORIN. Yes.

NINA. That's my late mother's country house. I was born there. I've spent my whole life on the shores of this lake and I know every islet in it.

TRIGORIN. Must be nice over at your place! (*Having spotted the gull.*) But what's this?

NINA. A gull. Konstantin Gavrilych killed it.

TRIGORIN. Lovely bird. Honestly, I don't feel like leaving. Look here, go and talk Irina Nikolaevna into staying. (*Jots a note in his notebook.*)[59]

NINA. What's that you're writing?

TRIGORIN. Just jotting down a note . . . A subject came to mind . . . (*Putting away the notebook.*) Subject for a short story: on the shores of a lake a young girl grows up, just like you; loves the lake, like a gull, is happy and free, like a gull. But by chance a man comes along, sees her, and, having nothing better to do, destroys her, just like this gull here.

    Pause. ARKADINA appears in a window.

ARKADINA. Boris Alekseevich, where are you?

---

59 Chekhov was against the indiscriminate use of notes in creative writing. "There's no reason to write down similes, tidy character sketches, or details of landscapes: they should appear of their own accord, whenever needed. But a bare fact, an unusual name, a technical term ought to be put down in a notebook; otherwise it will go astray and get lost."

TRIGORIN. Coming! (*Goes and takes a glance round at Nina; at the window, to Arkadina.*)

What?

ARKADINA. We're staying.

TRIGORIN exits into the house.

NINA (*Crosses down to the footlights; after a moment's thought*). It's a dream!

Curtain

~~~~~~~~

ACT THREE

Dining room in Sorin's house. Doors right and left. Sideboard. Cupboard with first-aid kit and medicine. Table center. Trunks and cardboard boxes; signs of preparation for a departure. TRIGORIN is eating lunch, MASHA stands by the table.

MASHA. I'm telling you all this because you're a writer. You can put it to use. I swear to you: if he'd wounded himself seriously, I wouldn't have gone on living another minute. Not that I'm not brave. I've gone and made up my mind. I'll rip this love out of my heart, I'll rip it up by the roots.

TRIGORIN. How so?

MASHA. I'm getting married. To Medvedenko.

TRIGORIN. That's that schoolteacher?

MASHA. Yes.

TRIGORIN. I don't see the necessity.

MASHA. Loving hopelessly, waiting and waiting for years on end for something . . . But once I'm married, there'll be no room for love, new problems will blot out the old one. And anyhow, you know, it makes a change. Shall we have another?

TRIGORIN. Aren't you overdoing it?

MASHA. Oh, go ahead! (*Pours out a shot for each.*) Don't look at me like that. Women drink more often than you think. A few drink openly, like me, but most of them do it on the sly. Yes. And it's always vodka or brandy. (*Clinks glasses.*) Here's to you! You're a nice man. I'm sorry you're going away.

They drink.[60]

TRIGORIN. If it were up to me, I wouldn't be leaving.

----

60 Vasily Kachalov wrote:

"Look, you know," Chekhov began, seeing how persistent I was, "when he, Trigorin, drinks vodka with Masha, I would definitely do it like this, definitely."

And with that he got up, adjusted his waistcoat, and awkwardly wheezed a couple of times.

"There you are, you know, I would definitely do it like that. When you've been sitting a long time, you always want to do that sort of thing . . ."

(*Shipovnik Almanac* 23 [1914])

MASHA. Then ask her to stay.

TRIGORIN. No, she won't stay now. Her son's been acting very tactlessly. First he tries to shoot himself,[61] and now I hear he intends to challenge me to a duel. And what for? He feuds and fusses, preaches about new forms . . . But there's room enough for everyone, isn't there? New and old—what's the point in shoving?

MASHA. Well, it's jealousy too. Though, that's no business of mine. (*Pause. YAKOV crosses left to right with a suitcase. NINA enters and stops by a window.*) My schoolteacher isn't very bright, but he's a decent sort, poor too, and he's awfully in love with me. I feel sorry for him. And I feel sorry for his poor old mother. Well, sir, please accept my best wishes. Think kindly of us. (*Shakes him firmly by the hand.*) Thanks a lot for your consideration. Do send me your book, and be sure there's an inscription. Only don't make it out "To dear madam," but simply "To Mariya, of no known family[62] and who lives in this world for no apparent reason." Good-bye. (*Exits.*)

NINA (*holding out her clenched fist to Trigorin*). Odds or evens?

TRIGORIN. Evens.

NINA (*sighing*). No. I've only got one bean in my hand. I was guessing whether to become an actress or not. If only someone would give me some advice.

---

61 The verb form in Russian makes it clear that he failed.

62 A common formula in police reports applied to vagrants without passports.

TRIGORIN. You can't give advice about things like that.

Pause.

NINA. We're parting and . . . most likely we'll never see one another again. Please take a keepsake of me, here, this little medallion. I had them engrave your initials . . . and on this other
side the title of your book: "Days and Nights."

TRIGORIN. How thoughtful! (*Kisses the medallion.*) A charming
gift!

NINA. Remember me from time to time.

TRIGORIN. I will. I will remember you as you were on that sunny
day—do *you* remember?—a week ago, when you were wearing
a brightly colored dress . . . We were having a long talk . . . and
something else, there was a white gull lying on the bench.

NINA (*pensively*). Yes, a gull . . . (*Pause.*) We can't go on talking,
someone's coming . . . Before you go, save two minutes for me,
please . . . (*Exits left.*)

   At that very moment ARKADINA enters right, as does
   SORIN in a tailcoat with a star pinned to his chest,[63]
   then YAKOV, preoccupied with packing.

ARKADINA. You should stay home, you old man. With that rheu-
matism of yours what are you doing riding around paying calls?
(*To Trigorin.*) Who went out just now? Nina?

---

63 The decoration is an appurtenance of his status as an Actual State Councillor.

TRIGORIN. Yes.

ARKADINA. *Excusez-moi*, we interrupted something . . . (*Sits down.*) I think everything's packed. I'm tired to death.

TRIGORIN (*reads the inscription on the medallion*). "Days and Nights," page 121, lines 11 and 12.

YAKOV (*clearing the table*). Do you want me to pack the fishing poles too?

TRIGORIN. Yes, I can use them again. But the books you can give away.

YAKOV. Yes, sir.

TRIGORIN (*to himself*). Page 121, lines 11 and 12. What is there in those lines? (*To Arkadina.*) Are there copies of my books anywhere in the house?

ARKADINA. In my brother's study, the corner bookcase.

TRIGORIN. Page 121 . . . (*Exits.*)

ARKADINA. Honestly, Petrusha, you ought to stay at home . . .

SORIN. You're leaving; with you gone it'll be boring at home . . .

ARKADINA And what's there to do in town?

SORIN. Nothing special, but even so. (*He laughs.*) They'll be laying the cornerstone for the town hall[64] and all the rest . . . Just for a

---

64 In the original, the new *zemstvo* building. .

couple of hours I'd like to stop feeling like a stick-in-the-mud,[65] I've been getting stale, like an old cigarette holder. I told them to send round my horses at one, we'll both go at the same time.

ARKADINA (*after a pause*). Oh, do stay here, don't be bored, don't catch cold. Look after my son. Keep an eye on him. Give him good advice.

Pause.

Now I've got to go and I still don't know how come Konstantin took a shot at himself. I suppose the main reason was jealousy, so the sooner I take Trigorin away from here, the better.

SORIN. How can I put this? There were other reasons too. Take my word for it, a man who's young, intelligent, living in the country, in the sticks, with no money, no position, no future. Nothing to keep him occupied. Gets ashamed of himself and alarmed by his own idleness. I love him dearly and he's very fond of me, but all the same, when all's said and done, he thinks he's unwanted at home, that he's a panhandler here, a charity case. Take my word for it, vanity . . .

ARKADINA. He's the cross I bear! (*Musing.*) He could get a desk job in the civil service, or something . . .

SORIN (*whistles a tune, then tentatively*). I think it would be best if you . . . gave him some money. First of all, he ought to be

---

65 Literally, this gudgeon's life (*peskarnaya zhizn*), a reference to Saltykov-Shchedrin's fable "The Wise Gudgeon," which deplores a conservative, philistine way of life.

dressed like a human being and all the rest. Just look, he's been wearing the same beat-up old frockcoat for the last three years, he has to go out without a topcoat . . . (*Laughs.*) Besides, it wouldn't hurt the boy to live it up a bit . . . Go abroad or something . . . It's not all that expensive.

ARKADINA. Even so . . . Possibly, I could manage the suit, but as for going abroad . . . No, at the moment I can't manage the suit either. (*Decisively.*) I have no money! (*SORIN laughs.*) None!

SORIN (*whistles a tune*). Yes, ma'am. Sorry, my dear, don't get angry. I believe you . . . You're a generous, selfless woman.

ARKADINA (*plaintively*). I have no money!

SORIN. If I had any money, take my word for it, I'd let him have it, but I haven't any, not a red cent. (*Laughs.*) The overseer snatches my whole pension from me, and wastes it on farming, livestock, beekeeping, and my money simply melts away. The bees die off, the cows die off, I can never get any horses . . .

ARKADINA. Yes, I do have some money, but I'm an actress, aren't I? My costumes alone are enough to ruin me.

SORIN. You're kind, affectionate . . . I respect you . . . Yes . . . But something's come over me again . . . (*Staggers.*) My head's spinning. (*Holds on to the table.*) I feel faint and all the rest.

ARKADINA (*alarmed*). Petrusha! (*Trying to hold him up.*) Petrusha, dear . . . (*Shouts.*) Help me! Help! (*Enter TREPLYOV, a bandage round his head, and MEDVEDENKO.*) He's fainting!

SORIN. Never mind, never mind . . . (*Smiles and drinks some water.*) It's all over . . . and all the rest.

TREPLYOV (*to his mother*). Don't be alarmed, Mama, it isn't serious. Uncle often gets like this these days. (*To his uncle.*) You ought to lie down for a while, Uncle.

SORIN. For a little while, yes . . . But all the same I'm driving to town . . . I'll go lie down and drive to town . . . Take it from me . . . (*He starts out, leaning on his stick.*)

MEDVEDENKO (*escorting him, holding his arm*). Here's a riddle: what goes on four legs in the morning, two at midday, three in the evening . . .[66]

SORIN (*laughs*). I know. And flat on its back at night. Thank you, I can walk on my own.

MEDVEDENKO. Now, now, don't show off! . . .

He and SORIN go out.

ARKADINA. He gave me such a fright!

TREPLYOV. Living in the country is bad for his health. He gets depressed. Now, Mama, if only you had a sudden fit of generosity and lent him a couple of thousand or so, he might be able to live in town all year long.

ARKADINA. I have no money. I'm an actress, not a banker.

Pause.

---

66 The classical Greek riddle the Sphinx offers Oedipus. The answer is *man*.

TREPLYOV. Mama, change my bandage. You do it so well.

ARKADINA (*gets iodoform and a drawerful of dressings from the first-aid cupboard*). The doctor's late.

TREPLYOV. He promised to be here by ten and it's already noon.

ARKADINA. Sit down. (*Removes the bandage from his head.*) Looks like a turban. Yesterday some tramp asked in the kitchen what your nationality was. It's almost completely healed. What's left is nothing. (*Kisses him on the head.*) And when I'm away, you won't do any more click-click?

TREPLYOV. No, Mama. It was a moment of insane desperation, when I lost control. It won't happen again. (*Kisses her hands.*) You've got wonderful hands. I remember long, long ago, when you were still working at the National Theatre[67]—I was a little boy then—there was a fight in our yard, a washerwoman who lived there got badly beaten up. Remember? She was picked up unconscious . . . You would go and see her, take her medicine, bathe her children in the washtub. Don't you remember?

ARKADINA. No. (*Putting on a fresh bandage.*)

TREPLYOV. At the time there were two ballerinas living in our building . . . They'd come and drink coffee with you . . .

ARKADINA. That I remember.

---

67 The official Imperial theaters in St. Petersburg and Moscow.

TREPLYOV. They were so religious.

Pause.

Just lately, these last few days, I love you every bit as tenderly and freely as when I was a child. Except for you, I've got no one left now. Only why, why do you give in to that man's influence?[68]

ARKADINA. You don't understand him, Konstantin. He's a person of the highest refinement.

TREPLYOV. But when they told him I was going to challenge him to a duel, his refinement didn't keep him from acting like a coward. He's going away. Retreating in disgrace!

ARKADINA. Don't be silly! I'm the one who's asked him to go away. Of course, I don't expect you to approve of our intimacy, but you're intelligent and sophisticated, I have the right to demand that you respect my independence.[69]

TREPLYOV. I do respect your independence, but you've got to let me be independent and treat that man any way I want.[70] The highest refinement! You and I are at one another's throats because of him, while he's somewhere in the drawing-room or the garden, laughing at us . . . cultivating Nina, trying to persuade her once and for all that he's a genius.

---

68 This phrase was excised by the censor and replaced by Chekhov with "why does that man have to come between us?"

69 These two lines were excised by the censor and replaced with "He'll go right now. I will ask him to leave here myself."

70 This line was excised by the censor.

ARKADINA. You enjoy hurting my feelings. I respect that man and must ask you not to say nasty things about him to my face.

TREPLYOV. But I don't respect him. You want me to treat him like a genius too. Well, pardon me, I cannot tell a lie, his writing makes me sick.

ARKADINA. That's jealousy. People with no talent but plenty of pretentions have nothing better to do than criticize really talented people. It's a comfort to them, I'm sure!

TREPLYOV (*sarcastically*). Really talented people! (*Angrily.*) I'm more talented than the lot of you put together, if it comes to that! (*Tears the bandage off his head.*) You dreary hacks hog the front-row seats in the arts and assume that the only legitimate and genuine things are what you do yourselves, so you suppress and stifle the rest! I don't believe in any of you! I don't believe in you or him!

ARKADINA. Mr. Avant-garde! . . .

TREPLYOV. Go back to your darling theater and act in your pathetic, third-rate plays.

ARKADINA. I have never acted in that kind of play. Leave me out of it! You haven't got what it takes to write a miserable vaudeville sketch. You bourgeois from Kiev! You panhandler!

TREPLYOV. You skinflint!

ARKADINA. You scarecrow! (*TREPLYOV sits down and weeps quietly.*) You nobody! (*Walking up and down in agitation.*)

Don't cry. You mustn't cry . . . (*She weeps.*) Don't do it . . . (*She kisses his forehead, cheeks, head.*) My darling boy, forgive me . . . Forgive your wicked mother. Forgive unhappy me.

TREPLYOV (*embraces her*). If only you knew! I've lost everything. She doesn't love me, I can't write anymore . . . I've lost all hope . . .

ARKADINA. Don't lose heart. Everything will turn out all right. He'll be leaving soon, she'll love you again. (*Wipes away his tears.*) There now. We're friends again.

TREPLYOV (*kisses her hands*). Yes, Mama.

ARKADINA (*tenderly*). Make friends with him too. There's no need for duels . . . Is there?

TREPLYOV. All right . . . Only, Mama, don't make me see him again. It's too hard for me . . . I can't deal with it . . . (*TRIGORIN enters.*) There he is . . . I'm going . . . (*He rapidly throws the first-aid kit into the cupboard.*) The Doctor will do my bandage later on . . .

TRIGORIN (*leafing through a book*). Page 121 . . . lines 11 and 12 . . . Aha! . . . (*Reads.*) "If ever my life is of use to you, come and take it."[71]

---

71 Nemirovich-Danchenko wrote:

While Chekhov was writing this play, the editors of *Russian Thought* sent him a bracelet charm in the shape of a book, on one side of which was engraved the title of his short story collection and on the other the numbers: p. 247, l. 6 and 7. The gift was anonymous. In his collection Anton Pavlovich read: "You are the most generous, the noblest of men. I am eternally grateful to you. If you ever need my life come and take it." It is from the story "Neighbors" (1892), in

*TREPLYOV picks the bandage up off the floor
and exits.*

ARKADINA (*after a glance at her watch*). The horses will be here soon.

TRIGORIN (*to himself*). If ever my life is of use to you, come and take it.

ARKADINA. You've got all your things packed, I hope?

TRIGORIN (*impatiently*). Yes, yes . . . (*Musing.*) How come this appeal from a pure spirit has sounded a note of sorrow and my heart aches so poignantly? . . . If ever my life is of use to you, come and take it. (*To Arkadina.*) Let's stay just one more day! (*ARKADINA shakes her head no.*) Let's stay!

ARKADINA. Darling, I know what's keeping you here. But do show some self-control. You're a little tipsy, sober up.

TRIGORIN. Then you be sober too, be understanding, reasonable, please, come to terms with this like a true friend . . . (*Squeezes her hand.*) You're capable of sacrifice . . . Be my friend, let me go.

---

which Grigory Vlasich says these words to his wife's brother. Anton Pavlovich vaguely surmised who had sent him this charm, and thought up an original way to send thanks and a reply: he had Nina give the same medallion to Trigorin and only changed the name of the book and the numbers. The answer arrived as intended at the first performance of *The Seagull*. The actors, of course, never suspected that, as they performed the play, they were simultaneously acting as letter-carriers."

(*Out of the Past* [1938])

ARKADINA (*extremely upset*). You're that far gone?

TRIGORIN. I'm attracted to her! Maybe this is just what I need.

ARKADINA. The love of some country girl? Oh, how little you know yourself!

TRIGORIN. Sometimes people walk in their sleep, look, I'm here talking to you, but it's as if I'm asleep and seeing her in my dreams . . . I've succumbed to sweet, wonderful visions . . . Let me go.

ARKADINA (*trembling*). No, no . . . I'm an ordinary woman, you mustn't talk to me that way . . . Don't tease me, Boris . . . It frightens me.

TRIGORIN. If you try, you can be extraordinary. A love that's young, charming, poetical, wafting me to a dream world — it's the one and only thing on this earth that can bring happiness. I've never yet experienced a love like that . . . When I was young I had no time, I was hanging around publishers' doorsteps, fighting off poverty . . . Now it's here, this love, it's come at last, luring me . . . What's the point of running away from it?

ARKADINA (*angrily*). You're out of your mind!

TRIGORIN. So what.

ARKADINA. You've all ganged up today to torture me! (*Weeps.*)

TRIGORIN (*puts his head in his hands*). She doesn't understand! She refuses to understand!

ARKADINA. Am I now so old and ugly that men don't think twice telling me about other women? (*Embraces and kisses him.*) Oh, you've gone crazy! My gorgeous, fabulous man . . . You're the last chapter in my life story! (*Kneels down.*) My joy, my pride, my blessedness . . . (*Embraces his knees.*) If you desert me for even a single hour, I won't survive. I'll go out of my mind, my incredible, magnificent man, my lord and master . . .

TRIGORIN. Somebody might come in. (*He helps her to rise.*)

ARKADINA. Let them, I'm not ashamed of my love for you. (*Kisses his hand.*) My precious, headstrong man, you want to do something reckless, but I won't have it, I won't let you . . . (*Laughs.*) You're mine . . . you're mine . . . And this forehead is mine, and these eyes are mine, and this beautiful silky hair is mine too . . . You're all mine. You're so talented, clever, our greatest living writer, you're Russia's only hope . . . You've got so much sincerity, clarity, originality, wholesome humor . . . With a single stroke you can pinpoint the most vital feature in a person or a landscape, your characters are so alive. Oh, no one can read you without going into ecstasy! You think this is soft soap?[72] Am I lying? Well, look into my eyes . . . look . . . Do I look like a liar? There, you see, I'm the only one who knows how to appreciate you; I'm the only one who tells you the truth, my darling, marvelous man . . . You will come? Won't you? You won't desert me?

---

72 *Finiam*, literally, incense; figuratively, gross flattery.

TRIGORIN. I've got no will of my own . . . I never had a will of my own . . . Wishy-washy, spineless, always giving in—how can a woman find that attractive? Take me, carry me off, but don't ever let me out of your sight . . .

ARKADINA (*to herself*). Now he is mine. (*Casually, as if nothing had happened.*) Of course, if you want to, you can stay. I'll go by myself, and you can come later, in a week's time. After all, what's your rush?

TRIGORIN. No, let's go together.

ARKADINA. If you say so. Together, whatever you like, together . . . (*Pause. TRIGORIN jots something in his note-book.*) What are you up to?

TRIGORIN. This morning I heard a good phrase: "the virgin grove" . . . It'll come in handy. (*Stretching.*) Which means, we're on our way? More train compartments, stations, lunch counters, fried food, smalltalk . . .

SHAMRAEV (*enters*). I have the melancholy honor of announcing that the horses are here. The time has come, dear lady, to go to the station; the train pulls in at two-o-five. By the way, Irina Nikolaevna, do me a favor, you won't forget to find out what's become of the actor Suzdaltsev these days? Is he alive? Is he well? Many's the drink we downed together once upon a time . . . In "The Great Mail Robbery" his acting was inimitable . . . I recall he was acting at the time in Elizavet-grad with the tragedian Izmailov, another remarkable character[73] . . . Don't rush yourself, dear lady, we can spare another five minutes. Once in some melodrama they were playing conspirators, and when they were suddenly caught, the line was supposed to go: "We've fallen into a trap," but Izmailov said, "We've trawlen into a flap" . . . (*Roars with laughter.*) Into a flap!

> *While he is speaking, YAKOV fusses around the luggage, a HOUSEMAID brings ARKADINA her hat, coat, parasol, gloves; everyone helps Arkadina to dress. The COOK peers in through the door left, and after waiting a bit he enters hesitantly. POLINA ANDREEVNA enters, then SORIN and MEDVEDENKO.*

POLINA ANDREEVNA (*with a tiny basket*). Here are some plums for your trip . . . Nice and ripe. You might want something for your sweet tooth.

ARKADINA. That's very kind of you, Polina Andreevna.

POLINA ANDREEVNA. Good-bye, my dear! If anything wasn't right, do forgive me. (*Weeps.*)

ARKADINA (*embraces her*). Everything was fine, just fine. Only you mustn't cry.

---

73 Actors invented by Chekhov. *The Great Mail Robbery* is F. A. Burdin's adaptation of the French melodrama *Le courrier de Lyon* (1850), by Eugène Lemoine-Moreau, Paul Siraudin, and Alfred Delacour, well known to Victorian English audiences as *The Lyons Mail*. As an adolescent in Taganrog, Chekhov had seen and loved this play.

POLINA ANDREEVNA. Time's running out for us!

ARKADINA. What can we do?

SORIN (*in an overcoat with a cape, wearing a hat and carrying a walking stick, enters from the door left; crosses the room*). Sister, it's time. You better not be late, when all's said and done. I'm going to get in. (*Exits.*)

MEDVEDENKO. And I'll go to the station on foot . . . to see you off. I'm a fast walker . . . (*He exits.*)

ARKADINA. Till we meet again, my dears . . . If we're alive and well, we'll see you again next summer . . . (*The HOUSEMAID, YAKOV, and the COOK kiss her hand.*) Don't forget me. (*Hands the COOK a ruble.*) Here's a ruble for the three of you.

COOK. Thank you kindly, ma'am. Have a pleasant trip! Mighty pleased to serve you!

YAKOV. God bless and keep you!

SHAMRAEV. Brighten our days with a little letter! Good-bye, Boris Alekseevich.

ARKADINA. Where's Konstantin? Tell him that I'm going. I've got to say good-bye. Well, think kindly of me. (*To Yakov.*) I gave a ruble to the cook. It's for the three of you.

> *Everyone goes out right. The stage is empty. Offstage*
> *there is the sort of noise that accompanies people*
> *seeing each other off. The HOUSEMAID returns to*
> *get the basket of plums from the table, and exits again.*

TRIGORIN (*returning*). I forgot my stick. I think it's out on the veranda. (*Crosses left and at the door runs into NINA, entering.*) Ah, it's you? We're leaving.

NINA. I felt we would meet again. (*Excited.*) Boris Alekseevich, I've made up my mind once and for all, the die is cast, I'm going on the stage. Tomorrow I'll be gone, I'm leaving my father, abandoning everything, starting a new life . . . I'm traveling like you . . . to Moscow. We shall meet there.

TRIGORIN (*glancing around*). Stay at the Slav Bazaar Hotel . . . Let me know the minute you're there . . . Molchanovka Street,[74] the Grokholsky Apartments . . . I'm in a hurry . . .

Pause.

NINA. Just one more minute.

TRIGORIN (*in an undertone*). You're so beautiful . . . Oh, how wonderful to think that we'll be seeing one another soon! (*She lays her head on his chest.*) I'll see these marvelous eyes again, that indescribably beautiful, tender smile . . . these delicate features, this look of angelic purity . . . My dearest . . . (*A prolonged kiss.*)

Curtain

---

74 *Slavyansky Bazar*, an elegant and fashionable hotel in central Moscow, rated one of the top three and much frequented by Chekhov. It was where Stanislavsky and Nemirovich-Danchenko held their epic lunch that resulted in the founding of the Moscow Art Theatre. Molchanovka is a street near Arbat Square in Moscow, in the center of the city, easy walking distance from the Slav Bazaar.

ACT FOUR

Between Acts Three and Four two years have elapsed.

*One of the drawing-rooms in Sorin's house, turned by Konstantin Treplyov into a workroom. Left and right doors, leading to inner rooms. Directly facing us, a glass door to the veranda. Besides the usual drawing-room furniture, in the right corner is a writing desk, near the left door a Turkish divan, a bookcase full of books, books on the windowsills, on chairs. —Evening. A single lamp with a shade is lit. Semi-darkness. We can hear the trees rustling and the wind wailing in the chimney. A WATCHMAN raps on a board.[75]
MEDVEDENKO and MASHA enter.*

MASHA (*shouts out*). Konstantin Gavrilych! Konstantin Gavrilych! (*Looking around.*) Nobody here. The old man never stops asking, where's Kostya, where's Kostya . . . Can't live without him . . .

MEDVEDENKO. Afraid to be left alone. (*Listening hard.*) What awful weather! For two whole days now.

MASHA (*igniting the flame in a lamp*). There are waves on the lake. Enormous ones.

---

75 On Russian country estates watchmen would make the rounds, tapping on a board to warn intruders of their presence.

MEDVEDENKO. It's dark outside. Somebody should tell them to pull down that stage in the garden. It stands there bare, unsightly, like a skeleton, and the scene curtain flaps in the wind. When I was going by last night, I thought somebody was on it, crying . . .

MASHA. You don't say . . .

Pause.

MEDVEDENKO. Let's go home, Masha!

MASHA (*shakes her head no*). I'll stay and spend the night here.

MEDVEDENKO (*pleading*). Masha, let's go! Our baby's starving, I'll bet!

MASHA. Don't be silly. Matryona will feed him.

Pause.

MEDVEDENKO. It's a shame. The third night now without his mother.

MASHA. You're getting tiresome. In the old days at least you used to talk philosophy, but now it's all baby, home, baby, home — that's all anybody hears out of you.

MEDVEDENKO. Let's go, Masha!

MASHA. Go yourself.

MEDVEDENKO. Your father won't give me any horses.

MASHA. He will. Ask him and he'll give you.

MEDVEDENKO. Maybe so, I'll ask. That means, you'll be home tomorrow?

MASHA (*takes snuff*). All right, tomorrow. You're a pest . . .

> *Enter TREPLYOV and POLINA ANDREEVNA;*
> *TREPLYOV is carrying pillows and a blanket, and*
> *POLINA ANDREEVNA bedclothes; they lay them on*
> *the Turkish divan, after which TREPLYOV goes to his*
> *desk and sits.*

MASHA. What's this for, Mama?

POLINA ANDREEVNA. Pyotr Nikolaevich asked for his bed to be made up in Kostya's room.

MASHA. Let me . . . (*Makes the bed.*)

POLINA ANDREEVNA (*sighs*). Old folks are like children . . . (*Walks over to the writing desk and, leaning on her elbows, looks at the manuscript.*)

Pause.

MEDVEDENKO. Well, I'm going. Good-bye, Masha. (*Kisses his wife's hand.*) Good-bye, Mama dear. (*Tries to kiss his mother-in-law's hand.*)

POLINA ANDREEVNA (*annoyed*). Well! Go if you're going.

MEDVEDENKO. Good-bye, Konstantin Gavrilych.

TREPLYOV silently offers his hand;
MEDVEDENKO exits.

POLINA ANDREEVNA (*looking at the manuscript*). Nobody had the slightest idea, Kostya, that you would turn into a real writer. And now look, thank God, they've started sending you money from the magazines. (*Runs her hand over his hair.*) And you're handsome now . . . Dear, good Kostya, be a little more affectionate to my Mashenka.

MASHA (*making the bed*). Leave him be, Mama.

POLINA ANDREEVNA (*to Treplyov*). She's a wonderful little thing. (*Pause.*) Women, Kostya, ask nothing more than an occasional look of kindness. I know from experience.

TREPLYOV gets up from behind the desk and
exits in silence.

MASHA. Now he's gone and got angry. You had to bring that up!

POLINA ANDREEVNA. I feel sorry for you, Mashenka.

MASHA. That's all I need!

POLINA ANDREEVNA. My heart bleeds for you. I do see everything, understand everything.

MASHA. It's all nonsense. Unrequited love—that's only in novels. Really silly. Just mustn't lose control or go on waiting for something, waiting for your ship to come in . . . If love ever burrows into your heart, you've got to get rid of it. They've just promised to transfer my husband to another school district. Once we've moved there—I'll forget all about it . . . I'll rip it out of my heart by the roots.

Two rooms away a melancholy waltz is played.

POLINA ANDREEVNA. Kostya's playing. That means he's depressed.

MASHA (*noiselessly makes a few waltz steps*). The main thing, Mama, is to have him out of sight. As soon as they transfer my Semyon, then believe you me, I'll forget in a month. This is all so silly.

The door left opens. DORN and MEDVEDENKO
wheel in SORIN, in his armchair.

MEDVEDENKO. I've got six at home now. And flour almost two kopeks a pound.

DORN. It gets you going in circles.

MEDVEDENKO. It's all right for you to laugh. You've got more money than you could shake a stick at.

DORN. Money? After thirty years of practice, my friend, on constant call night and day, when I couldn't call my soul my own, all I managed to scrape together was two thousand; besides, I blew it all on my recent trip abroad. I haven't a penny.

MASHA (*to her husband*). Haven't you gone?

MEDVEDENKO (*apologetically*). How? If they don't give me horses!

MASHA (*bitterly annoyed, in an undertone*). I wish I'd never set eyes on you!

The wheelchair is halted in the left half of the room; POLINA ANDREEVNA, MASHA, and DORN sit down beside it; MEDVEDENKO, saddened, moves away to one side.

DORN. So many changes around here, I must say! They've turned the drawing-room into a study.

MASHA. It's more comfortable for Konstantin Gavrilych to work here. Whenever he likes, he can go out in the garden and think.

The WATCHMAN taps his board.

SORIN. Where's my sister?

DORN. Gone to the station to meet Trigorin. She'll be back any minute.

SORIN. If you found it necessary to write for my sister to come here, it means I'm seriously ill. (*After a silence.*) A fine state of affairs, I'm seriously ill, but meanwhile they won't give me any medicine.

DORN. And what would you like? Aspirin? Bicarbonate? Quinine?

SORIN. Uh-oh, here comes the philosophizing. Oh, what an affliction! (*Nodding his head towards the divan.*) That made up for me?

POLINA ANDREEVNA. For you, Pyotr Nikolaevich.

SORIN. Thank you.

DORN (*sings*). "The moon sails through the midnight sky . . ."[76]

SORIN. There's this subject for a story I want to give Kostya. The title should be: "The Man Who Wanted to." "*L'Homme qui a voulu.*"[77] In my youth I wanted to be an author—and wasn't; wanted to speak eloquently—and spoke abominably (*mimicking himself*) "and so on and so forth, this, that, and the other . . ." and in summing up used to ramble on and on, even broke out in a sweat; wanted to get married—and didn't; always wanted to live in town—and now am ending my life in the country and all the rest.

DORN. Wanted to become a senior civil servant—and did.

SORIN (*laughs*). That I never tried for. It came all by itself.

DORN. Complaining of life at age sixty-two is, you must agree— not very gracious.

SORIN. What a pigheaded fellow. Don't you realize, I'd like to live.

DORN. That's frivolous. By the laws of nature every life must come to an end.

---

76 Beginning of a serenade by K. S. Shilovsky, popular at the time; its sheet music had gone through ten printings by 1882.

77 Chekhov may have been familiar with a series of comic monologues by the eccentric French writer Charles Cros, called *L'Homme Qui*, published between 1877 and 1882.

SORIN. You argue like someone who's had it all. You've had it all and so you don't care about life, it doesn't matter to you. But even you will be afraid to die.

DORN. Fear of death is an animal fear . . . Have to repress it. A conscious fear of death is only for those who believe in life ever-lasting, which scares them because of their sins. But in the first place, you don't believe in religion, and in the second—what kind of sins have you got? You worked twenty-seven years in the Department of Justice—that's all.

SORIN (*laughs*). Twenty-eight.

TREPLYOV enters and sits on the footstool at Sorin's feet. MASHA never takes her eyes off him the whole time.

DORN. We're keeping Konstantin Gavrilovich from working.

TREPLYOV. No, not at all.

Pause.

MEDVEDENKO. Might I ask, Doctor, which town abroad you liked most?

DORN. Genoa.

TREPLYOV. Why Genoa?

DORN. The superb crowds in the streets there. In the evening when you leave your hotel, the whole street is teeming with people. Then you slip into the crowd, aimlessly, zigzagging this way and that, you live along with it, you merge with it psychically and you start to believe that there may in fact be a universal soul, much like the one that Nina Zarechnaya acted in your play once.[78] By the way, where is Miss Zarechnaya these days? Where is she and how is she?

TREPLYOV. She's all right, I suppose.

DORN. I'm told she seems to be leading a rather peculiar life. What's that all about?

TREPLYOV. That, Doctor, is a long story.

DORN. Then you shorten it.

Pause.

TREPLYOV. She ran away from home and went off with Trigorin. You know about that?

DORN. I do.

TREPLYOV. She had a baby. The baby died. Trigorin fell out of love with her and returned to his previous attachment, as might have been expected. In fact, he had never given up the previous one but, in his spineless way, somehow maintained both of them. So far as I can make out from my information, Nina's private life has not been a roaring success.

---

78 Dr. Dorn's pleasure in fleeing the constraints of individual personality into multiple personality echoes Baudelaire: "The pleasure of being in crowds is a mysterious expression of the delight in the multiplication of numbers."

DORN. And the stage?

TREPLYOV. Even worse, it would seem. She made her debut outside Moscow at a summer theater, then toured the provinces. In those days I was keeping track of her and for a while wherever she was, I was there too. She would tackle the big roles, but her acting was crude, tasteless, her voice singsong and her gestures wooden. There were moments when she showed some talent at screaming or dying, but they were only moments.

DORN. In other words, she does have *some* talent?

TREPLYOV. It was hard to tell. I suppose she has. I saw her, but she didn't want to see me, and her maid wouldn't let me into her hotel room. I understood her mood and didn't insist on meeting. (*Pause.*) What else is there to tell you? Later, by the time I'd returned home, I would get letters from her. The letters were clever, affectionate, interesting; she never complained, but I felt that she was deeply unhappy; not a line but revealed frayed, strained nerves. And a somewhat deranged imagination. She would sign herself The Gull. In that play of Pushkin's, the miller says that he's a raven;[79] that's how she'd keep repeating in all her letters that she was a gull.[80] She's here now.

DORN. What do you mean here?

79 *Rusalka* (*The Naiad* or *Nixie*), a fragment of a verse drama by Aleksandr Pushkin (1799–1837), written sometime between 1826 and 1832; the story of a poor miller's daughter, seduced and abandoned by a prince. She drowns herself and turns into a water nymph, while her father goes mad and calls himself "the local raven." The tale was turned into an opera by A. S. Dargomyzhsky.

80 Since there are no definite or indefinite articles in Russian, this could also be translated "she is *the* gull."

TREPLYOV. In town, at the railway hotel. About five days now she's been staying in a room there. I've been to see her, and Marya Ilyinishna drove over, but she won't receive anyone. Semyon Semyonych claims that yesterday after dinner he saw her in a field, a mile and a half from here.

MEDVEDENKO. Yes, I did see her. Heading for town. I bowed, asked her how come she didn't pay us a visit. She said she would.

TREPLYOV. She won't. (*Pause.*) Her father and stepmother have disowned her. They've set up watchmen all over so that she can't even get near the estate. (*Moves to the desk with the Doctor.*) How easy, Doctor, to be a philosopher on paper and how hard it is in fact!

SORIN. Splendid girl she was.

DORN. What's that again?

SORIN. Splendid girl, I said, she was. District Attorney Sorin was even a little bit in love with her for a while.

DORN. Old Casanova.[81]

SHAMRAEV's laugh is heard.

POLINA ANDREEVNA. I think our folks are back from the station . . .

---

81 Literally, "old Lovelace," the voluptuary hero of Samuel Richardson's *Clarissa* (1748), whose sole purpose in life is to seduce the heroine. Its Russian version was hugely popular in the late eighteenth century, even among those who, like Tatyana's mother in *Yevgeny Onegin*, didn't read it. ("She loved Richardson / Not because she preferred Grandison to Lovelace; / But in the old days Princess Alina, / Her Moscow cousin, / Had often rambled on about them to her" [Act II, scene 30].) "Lovelace" gradually became a standard term for a philanderer.

TREPLYOV. Yes, I hear Mama.

*Enter ARKADINA, TRIGORIN, followed by
SHAMRAEV.*

SHAMRAEV (*entering*). We're all growing old, weather-beaten by the elements, but you, dear lady, are just as young as ever . . . Colorful jacket, vivacity . . . grace . . .

ARKADINA. You want to put a hex on me again, you tiresome man!

TRIGORIN (*to Sorin*). Good evening, Pyotr Nikolaevich! How come you're still under the weather? That's not good! (*Having seen Masha, jovially.*) Marya Ilyinishna!

MASHA. You recognized me? (*Shakes his hand.*)

TRIGORIN. Married?

MASHA. Long ago.

TRIGORIN. Happy? (*Exchanges bows with DORN and MEDVE-DENKO, then hesitantly walks over to Treplyov.*) Irina Niko-laevna said that you've let bygones be bygones and no longer hold a grudge.

TREPLYOV extends his hand to him.

ARKADINA (*to her son*). Look, Boris Alekseevich brought the magazine with your new story.

TREPLYOV (*accepting the magazine, to Trigorin*). Thank you. Very kind of you.

They sit down.

TRIGORIN. Your fans send you their best wishes. In Petersburg and Moscow, mostly, they're starting to take an interest in you, and they're always asking me about you. Standard questions: what's he like, how old, dark or fair. For some reason they all think you're not young anymore. And nobody knows your real name, since you publish under a pseudonym. You're a mystery, like the Man in the Iron Mask.[82]

TREPLYOV. You staying long?

TRIGORIN. No, tomorrow I think I'll go to Moscow. Have to. I'm tripping over myself to finish a novella, and after that I've promised to contribute something to an anthology. In short— the same old story.

While they're conversing, ARKADINA and POLINA ANDREEVNA put a card table in the middle of the room and open it up; SHAMRAEV lights candles, arranges chairs. They get a lotto set[83] from a cupboard.

---

82 A mysterious political prisoner under Louis XIV, whose face was hidden by an iron mask. He was first mentioned in the *Mémoires secrets pour servir à l'histoire de Perse* (Amsterdam, 1745–1746), where he was alleged to be Louis's bastard. He is best known from *Le Vicomte de Bragelonne* (1848–1850), the third of Alexandre Dumas's musketeer novels, in which he is supposed to be Louis's twin.

83 An Italian import, known to Americans as Bingo, the game became fashionable in northern Russia in the 1840s and was briefly banned as a form of gambling. It was the common evening diversion on Chekhov's farm at Melikhovo.

TRIGORIN. The weather's given me a rude welcome. Ferocious wind. Tomorrow morning, if it's calmed down, I'll head out to the lake and do some fishing. By the way, I have to take a look round the garden and the place where— remember?—your play was performed. I've come up with a theme, just have to refresh my memory on the setting of the action.

MASHA (*to her father*). Papa, let my husband borrow a horse! He has to get home.

SHAMRAEV (*mimicking*). Horse ... home ... (*Severely.*) You saw yourself: they've just been to the station. They're not to go out again.

MASHA. But there must be other horses ... (*Seeing that her father is not forthcoming, she waves her hand dismissively.*) I don't want anything to do with either of you ...

MEDVEDENKO. I'll go on foot, Masha. Honestly.

POLINA ANDREEVNA (*sighs*). On foot in weather like this ... (*Sits at the card table.*) If you please, ladies and gentlemen.

MEDVEDENKO. It's really only four miles in all ... Good-bye ... (*Kisses his wife's hand.*) Good-bye, Mama dear. (*His mother-in-law reluctantly extends her hand for him to kiss.*) I wouldn't have disturbed anybody, except that the baby ... (*Bows to them all.*) Good-bye ... (*He exits apologetically.*)

SHAMRAEV. Never fear, he'll get there. He's nobody special.

POLINA ANDREEVNA (*raps on the table*). If you please, ladies and gentlemen. Let's not waste time, they'll be calling us to supper soon.

SHAMRAEV, MASHA, and DORN sit at the table.

ARKADINA (*to Trigorin*). When the long autumn evenings draw on, they play lotto here. Come and have a look: the old-fashioned lotto set our late mother used to play with us when we were children. Wouldn't you like to play a round with us before supper? (*Sits at the table with Trigorin.*) The game's a bore, but once you get used to it, you don't mind. (*Deals three cards to each.*)

TREPLYOV (*leafing through the magazine*). His own story he's read, but on mine he hasn't even cut the pages. (*Puts the magazine on the desk, then starts for the door left; moving past his mother, he kisses her head.*)

ARKADINA. What about you, Kostya?

TREPLYOV. Sorry, I don't feel up to it . . . I'm going for a walk. (*Exits.*)

ARKADINA. The stakes are ten kopeks. Ante up for me, Doctor.

DORN. Your wish is my command.

MASHA. Everyone's ante'd up? I'm starting . . . Twenty-two!

ARKADINA. Got it.

MASHA. Three! . . .

DORN. Righto.

MASHA. Got three? Eight! Eighty-one! Ten!

SHAMRAEV. Not so fast.

ARKADINA. The reception they gave me in Kharkov, goodness gracious, my head's still spinning from it!

MASHA. Thirty-four!

A melancholy waltz is played offstage.

ARKADINA. The students organized an ovation . . . Three baskets of flowers, two bouquets, and look at this . . . (*Unpins a brooch from her bosom and throws it on the table.*)

SHAMRAEV. Yes, that's something, all right . . .

MASHA. Fifty! . . .

DORN. Just plain fifty?

ARKADINA. I was wearing a gorgeous outfit . . . Say what you like, when it comes to dressing I'm nobody's fool.

POLINA ANDREEVNA. Kostya's playing. The poor boy's depressed.

SHAMRAEV. The newspaper reviewers give him a hard time.

MASHA. Seventy-seven!

ARKADINA. Who cares about them.

TRIGORIN. He hasn't had any luck. His writing still can't manage to find its proper voice. There's something odd, indefinite about it, sometimes it's like gibberish . . . Not one living character.

MASHA. Eleven!

ARKADINA (*looking round at Sorin*). Petrusha, are you bored? (*Pause.*) He's asleep.

DORN. Sleep comes to the senior civil servant.

MASHA. Seven! Ninety!

TRIGORIN. If I lived on an estate like this, by a lake, you think I'd write? I'd kick this addiction and do nothing but fish.

MASHA. Twenty-eight!

TRIGORIN. To catch a chub or a perch—that's my idea of heaven!

DORN. Well, I have faith in Konstantin Gavrilych. There's something there! There's something there! He thinks in images, his stories are colorful, striking, and I have a real fondness for them. It's just a pity he doesn't have well-defined goals. He creates an impression, and leaves it at that, and of course by itself an impression doesn't get you very far. Irina Nikolaevna, are you glad your son's a writer?

ARKADINA. Imagine, I still haven't read him. Never any time.

MASHA. Twenty-six!

TREPLYOV *quietly enters and goes to his desk.*

SHAMRAEV (*to Trigorin*). Hey, Boris Alekseevich, that thing of yours is still here.

TRIGORIN. What thing?

SHAMRAEV. A while back Konstantin Gavrilych shot a gull, and you asked me to have it stuffed.

TRIGORIN. Don't remember. (*Thinking about it.*) Don't remember!

MASHA. Sixty-six! One!

TREPLYOV (*throws open the window, listens*). So dark! I can't understand how it is I feel so uneasy.

ARKADINA. Kostya, shut the window, it's drafty.

TREPLYOV closes the window.

MASHA. Eighty-eight!

TRIGORIN. It's my game, ladies and gentlemen.

ARKADINA (*merrily*). Bravo! Bravo!

SHAMRAEV. Bravo!

ARKADINA. This man has the most incredible luck, any time, any place. (*Rises.*) And now let's have a bite to eat: Our celebrity didn't have dinner today. After supper we'll resume our game. (*To her son.*) Kostya, put down your writing, we're eating.

TREPLYOV. I don't want any, Mama. I'm not hungry.

ARKADINA. You know best. (*Wakes Sorin.*) Petrusha, supper-time! (*Takes Shamraev's arm.*) I'll tell you about my reception in Kharkov . . .

POLINA ANDREEVNA *blows out the candles on the
table, then she and* DORN *wheel out the armchair.
Everyone goes out the door left. Only* TREPLYOV
remains alone on stage at the writing desk.

TREPLYOV (*prepares to write; scans what he's already written*).
I've talked so much about new forms, but now I feel as if I'm
gradually slipping into routine myself. (*Reads.*) "The poster on
the fence proclaimed . . . A pale face, framed by dark hair . . ."
Proclaimed, framed . . . It's trite.[84] (*Scratches it out.*) I'll start
with the hero waking to the sound of rain, and get rid of all the
rest. The description of the moonlit night's too long and con-
trived. Trigorin has perfected a technique for himself, it's easy
for him . . . He has a shard of broken bottle glisten on the dam
and a black shadow cast by the millwheel—and there's your
moonlit night readymade.[85] But I've got to have the flickering
light, and the dim twinkling of the stars, and the distant strains
of a piano, dying away in the still, fragrant air . . . It's excruciating. (*Pause.*) Yes, I'm more and more convinced that the point
isn't old or new forms, it's to write and not think about form,
because it's flowing freely out of your soul. (*Someone knocks
at the window closest to the desk.*) What's that? (*Looks out the*

84 Chekhov used the same words in criticizing a story by Zhirkevich. "Nowadays
ladies are the only writers who use 'the poster proclaimed,' 'a face framed by hair.'"

85 Compare Chekhov's story "The Wolf" (1886): "On the weir, drenched in moon-
light, there was not a trace of shadow; in the middle the neck of a broken bottle shone
like a star. The two millwheels, half sheltered in the shade of an outspread willow,
looked angry and bad-tempered . . ." In a letter to his brother (May 10, 1886), he offers
it as a facile technique.

window.) Can't see anything . . . (*Opens the glass door and looks into the garden*.) Somebody's running down the steps. (*Calls out*.) Who's there? (*Goes out; he can be heard walking rapidly along the veranda; in a few seconds he returns with NINA ZARECHNAYA*.) Nina! Nina! (*NINA lays her head on his chest and sobs with restraint*.) (*Moved*.) Nina! Nina! it's you . . . you . . . I had a premonition, all day my heart was aching terribly. (*Removes her hat and knee-length cloak*.)[86] Oh, my sweet, my enchantress, she's here! We won't cry, we won't.

NINA. There's somebody here.

TREPLYOV. Nobody.

NINA. Lock the doors, or they'll come in.

TREPLYOV. No one will come in.

NINA. I know Irina Nikolaevna is here. Lock the doors.

TREPLYOV (*locks the door at right with a key, crosses left*). This one has no lock. I'll put a chair against it. (*Sets a chair against the door*.) Don't be afraid, no one will come in.

NINA (*stares fixedly at his face*). Let me look at you. (*Looking round*.) Warm, pleasant . . . This used to be a drawing-room. Have I changed a great deal?

TREPLYOV. Yes . . . You've lost weight, and your eyes are bigger. Nina, it feels so strange to be seeing you. How come you didn't

---

86 In the original, *talma*. A quilted, knee-length cloak with a wide, turned-down collar and silk lining, named after the French tragedian François Joseph Talma.

let me in? How come you didn't show up before now? I know you've been living here almost a week . . . I've been over to your place several times every day, stood beneath your window like a beggar.

NINA. I was afraid you hated me. Every night I have the same dream that you look at me and don't recognize me. If you only knew! Ever since my arrival I keep coming here . . . to the lake. I was at your house lots of times and couldn't make up my mind to go in. Let's sit down. (*They sit.*) We'll sit and we'll talk and talk. It's nice here, warm, cozy . . . Do you hear—the wind? There's a passage in Turgenev: "Happy he who on such a night sits beneath his roof, and has a warm corner."[87] I'm a gull . . . No, that's wrong. (*Rubs her forehead.*) What was I on about? Yes . . . Turgenev . . . "And the Lord help all homeless wanderers . . ." Never mind. (*Sobs.*)

TREPLYOV. Nina, you still . . . Nina!

NINA. Never mind, it makes me feel better . . . For two years now I haven't cried. Late last night I went to look at the garden, to see if our stage was still there. And it's standing to this day. I burst into tears for the first time in two years, and I felt relieved, my heart grew lighter. You see, I've stopped crying. (*Takes him by the hand.*) And so, now you're a writer. You're a writer, I'm an actress . . . We've both fallen into the maelstrom[88] . . . I used to

---

87 The last sentence is slightly misquoted from the epilogue of Turgenev's novel *Rudin* (1856).

88 *Omut* can also be translated as "millrace," which would connect back to the

live joyously, like a child—wake up in the morning and start to sing; I loved you, dreamed of fame, and now? First thing tomorrow morning I go to Yelets,[89] third class . . . traveling with peasants, and in Yelets art-loving businessmen will pester me with their propositions. A sordid kind of life!

TREPLYOV. Why Yelets?

NINA. I took an engagement for the whole winter. Time to go.

TREPLYOV. Nina, I cursed you, hated you, tore up your letters and photographs, but every moment I realized that my soul is bound to you forever. I haven't the power to stop loving you. From the time I lost you and began publishing, life for me has been unbearable—I'm in pain . . . My youth was suddenly somehow snatched away, and I felt as if I'd been living on this earth for ninety years. I appeal to you, kiss the ground you walk on; wherever I look, everywhere your face rises up before me, that caressing smile that shone on me in the best years of my life . . .

NINA (*perplexed*). Why does he say such things, why does he say such things?

TREPLYOV. I'm alone, unwarmed by anyone's affection. I'm cold as in a dungeon, and, no matter what I write, it's all arid,

---

Rusalka imagery. In Act Three of *Uncle Vanya*, it is translated as "millrace."

89 The Des Moines of tsarist Russia, a rapidly growing provincial trade center in the Oryol *guberniya*, south of Tula, noted for its grain elevators, tanneries, and brickyard, with a population of 52,000.

stale, gloomy. Stay here, Nina, I beg you, or let me go with you! (*NINA quickly puts on her hat and cloak.*) Nina, why? For God's sake, Nina . . . (*Watches her put on her wraps.*)

Pause.

NINA. My horses are standing at the gate. Don't see me out, I'll manage by myself . . . (*Tearfully.*) Give me some water . . .

TREPLYOV (*gives her something to drink*). Where are you off to now?

NINA. To town. (*Pause.*) Is Irina Nikolaevna here?

TREPLYOV. Yes . . . On Thursday Uncle wasn't well, we wired for her to come.

NINA. Why do you tell me you'd kiss the ground I walk on? I should be killed. (*Leans over the desk.*) I feel so tired! Have to get some rest . . . rest! (*Lifts her head.*) I'm a gull . . . That's wrong, I'm an actress. Ah, yes! (*Having heard Arkadina's and Trigorin's laughter, she listens, then runs to the door left and peeks through the keyhole.*) He's here too . . . (*Returning to Treplyov.*) Ah, yes . . . Never mind . . . Yes . . . He had no faith in the theater, he'd laugh at my dreams, and little by little I lost faith in it too, lost heart . . . But then the anxiety over our affair, jealousy, constant worrying about the baby . . . I became petty, trivial, acted mindlessly . . . I didn't know what to do with my hands, didn't know how to stand on stage, couldn't control my voice. You can't imagine what that's like, when you realize your acting is terrible. I'm a gull. No, that's wrong . . . Remember, you shot down a gull? By chance a man comes along, sees, and with nothing better to do destroys . . . Subject for a short story. That's wrong . . . (*Rubs her forehead.*) What was I saying? . . . I was talking about the stage. I'm not like that now . . . Now I'm a real actress, I like acting, I enjoy it, I'm intoxicated when I'm on stage and feel that I'm beautiful. And now that I'm living here, I go walking and walking and thinking and thinking and feel every day my spirit is growing stronger . . . Now I know, understand, Kostya, that in our work—it doesn't matter whether we act or we write—the main thing isn't fame, glamour, the things I dreamed about, it's knowing how to endure. I know how to shoulder my cross and I have faith. I have faith and it's not so painful for me, and when I think about my calling, I'm not afraid of life.

TREPLYOV (*mournfully*). You've found your path, you know where you're going, but I'm still drifting in a chaos of daydreams and images, without knowing what or whom it's for. I have no faith and I don't know what my calling is.[90]

NINA (*listening hard*). Ssh . . . I'm going. Good-bye. When I become a great actress, come to the city and have a look at me. Promise? But now . . . (*Squeezes his hand.*) Now it's late. I'm dead on my feet . . . I'm famished, I'd like a bite to eat . . .

TREPLYOV. Stay here, I'll bring you some supper . . .

---

90 From Chekhov's notebook: "Treplyov has no well-defined aims, and this is what destroyed him. His talent destroyed him. He says to Nina at the end: 'You have found your path, you are saved, but I am ruined.' "

NINA. No, no . . . Don't show me out, I'll manage by myself . . . My horses are close by . . . That means, she brought him with her? So what, it doesn't matter. When you see Trigorin, don't say anything to him . . . I love him. I love him even more than before . . . Subject for a short story . . . I love, love passionately, love to desperation. It used to be nice. Kostya! Remember? What a bright, warm, joyful, pure life, what feelings—feelings like tender, delicate flowers . . . Remember? . . . (*Recites.*) "Humans, lions, eagles, and partridges, antlered deer, geese, spiders, silent fishes that inhabit the waters, starfish, and those beings invisible to the naked eye,—in short, all living things, all living things, all living things, having completed the doleful cycle, are now extinct . . . Already thousands of centuries have passed since the earth bore any living creature, and this pale moon to no avail doth light her lamp. No more does the meadow awake to the cries of cranes, and the mayflies are no longer to be heard in the linden groves . . ." (*Embraces Treplyov impulsively and runs to the glass door.*)

TREPLYOV (*after a pause*). I hope nobody runs into her in the garden and tells Mama. It might distress Mama . . . (*Over the course of two minutes, he silently tears up all his manuscripts and throws them under the desk, then unlocks the door and exits.*)

DORN (*trying to open the door left*). Funny. Door seems to be locked . . . (*Enters and puts the chair in its proper place.*) Obstacle course.

Enter ARKADINA, POLINA ANDREEVNA,
followed by YAKOV with bottles and MASHA, then
SHAMRAEV and TRIGORIN.

ARKADINA. Put the red wine and the beer for Boris Alekseevich here on the table. We'll drink while we play. Let's sit down, ladies and gentlemen.

POLINA ANDREEVNA (*to Yakov*). And bring the tea now. (*Lights the candles, sits at the card table.*)

SHAMRAEV (*leads Trigorin to the cupboard*). Here's that thing I was talking about before . . . (*Gets a stuffed gull out of the cupboard.*) You ordered it.

TRIGORIN (*staring at the gull*). Don't remember! (*Thinking about it.*) Don't remember!

A shot offstage right; everyone shudders.

ARKADINA (*alarmed*). What's that?

DORN. Nothing. I suppose something exploded in my first-aid kit. Don't worry. (*Exits through the door right, returns in a few seconds.*) That's what it is. A vial of ether exploded. (*Sings.*) "Once again I stand bewitched before thee . . ."

ARKADINA (*sitting at the table*). Phew, I was terrified. It reminded me of the time . . . (*Hides her face in her hands.*) Things even went black before my eyes . . .

DORN (*leafing through the magazine, to Trigorin*). About two months ago there was a certain article published in here . . . a letter from America, and I wanted to ask you, among other things . . . (*takes Trigorin round the waist and leads him down to the footlights*) because I'm very interested in this matter . . . (*Lowering his voice.*) Take Irina Nikolaevna somewhere away from here. The fact is, Konstantin Gavrilovich *has* shot himself . . .

Curtain

VARIANTS

These lines appeared in the censorship's copy (Cens.), the first publication in the journal *Russian Thought* (*Russkaya Mysl*, 1896) (RT), and the 1897 edition of Chekhov's plays (1897).

ACT ONE

page 72 / *After*: And tobacco? — Yesterday, ma'am, I had to get some flour, we look for the bag, high and low, and beggars had stolen it. Had to pay fifteen kopeks for another one. (Cens.)

page 73 / *Before*: Talk to my father yourself, because I won't. — MASHA. Tell him yourself. The barn is full of millet now, and he says that if it weren't for the dogs thieves would carry it off. TREPLYOV. To hell with him and his millet! (Cens.)

page 73 / *After*: I never get my way in the country—it's all millet one time, dogs another, no horses another, because they've gone to the mill and so on and so forth. (Cens.)

page 76 / *Before*: You've got it in your head — Horace said: *genus irritabile vatum.*[1] (Cens., RT)

page 79 / *After*: when all's said and done ... — Once, about ten years ago, I published an article about trial lawyers, I just remembered, and, you know, it was pleasant, and meanwhile when I begin to remember that I worked twenty-eight years in the Justice Department, it's the other way round, I'd rather not think about it ... (*Yawns.*) (Cens.)

page 85 / *Before*: TREPLYOV *enters from behind the platform.*

MEDVEDENKO (*to Sorin*). And before Europe achieves results, humanity, as Flammarion[2] writes, will perish as a consequence of the cooling of the earth's hemispheres.

SORIN. God bless us.

MASHA (*offering her snuffbox to Trigorin*). Do have some! You're always so silent, or do you ever talk?

TRIGORIN. Yes, I talk sometimes. (*Takes snuff.*) Disgusting. How can you!

MASHA. Well, you've got a nice smile. I suppose you're a simple man. (Cens.)

page 90 / *After*: I didn't mean to offend him. —

NINA (*peering out from behind the curtain*). Is it over already? We won't be going on?

---

1 Latin: "Touchy is the tribe of poets," from Horace's *Epistles*, II, 2.

2 Camille Flammarion (1842–1925), French astronomer, prolific author of books on popular science, including *The Plurality of Inhabited Worlds* (1890). His astronomical fantasies inspired some of the features in Treplyov's play.

ARKADINA. The author left. I suppose it is over. Come on out, my dear, and join us.

NINA. Right away. (*Disappears.*)

MEDVEDENKO (*to Masha*). It all depends on the substantiality of psychic matter and there's no basis. (Cens.)

page 91 / *After*: but in those days he was irresistible. —

Polina Andreevna weeps quietly.

SHAMRAEV (*reproachfully*). Polina, Polina . . .

POLINA ANDREEVNA. Never mind . . . Forgive me . . . I suddenly got so depressed! (Cens.)

page 92 / *After*: Yes. —

SHAMRAEV. Bream and pike, for the most part. There are pike-perch as well, but not many. (Cens.)

page 94 / *After*: Credit where credit's due. —

MEDVEDENKO. A deplorable manifestation of atavism, worthy of the attention of Lombroso.[3]

DORN (*teasing*). "Lombroso" . . . You can't live without pedantic words. (Cens.)

page 94 / *After*: (*Takes him by the arm.*) — In some play there's a line: "Come to your senses, old man!" (Cens.)

page 97 / *Replace*: And will you all please leave me in peace! Stay here! Don't come after me!

---

3 Cesare Lombroso (1856–1909), Italian criminologist, who published widely on the subject of decadence, sexual abnormality, and insanity; he believed that criminals and psychopaths could be identified by physical traits.

with: **MASHA**. On what? My father will tell you that all the horses are busy.

TREPLYOV (*angrily*). He hasn't got the right! I don't keep anyone from living, so they can leave me in peace. (Cens.)

ACT TWO

page 99 / *After*: you don't live . . . —

MASHA. My mamma brought me up like that girl in the fairy tale who lived in a flower. I don't know how to do anything. (Cens.)

page 101 / *After*: just consider me and Trigorin. — I didn't pick out Boris Alekseevich, didn't lay siege, didn't enthrall, but when we met, everything in my head went topsy-turvy, my dears, and things turned green before my eyes. I used to stand and look at him and cry. I mean it, I'd howl and howl. What kind of master plan is that? (Cens.)

page 102 / *After*: "At Sea" by Maupassant, sweetheart. —

MEDVEDENKO. Never read it.

DORN. You only read what you don't understand.

MEDVEDENKO. Whatever books I can get I read.

DORN. All you read is Buckle and Spencer,⁴ but you've got no

---

4 Henry Thomas Buckle (1821–1862), whose *History of Civilization in England* was translated into Russian in 1861, posited that skepticism was the handmaiden of progress and that religion retards the advance of civilization. Herbert Spencer (1820–1903) was an English philosopher and sociologist whose works were extensively translated into Russian. Buckle and Spencer's materialist views were much appreciated by pro-

more knowledge than a night watchman. According to you, the heart is made out of cartilage and the earth is held up by whales.

MEDVEDENKO. The earth is round.

DORN. Why do you say that so diffidently?

MEDVEDENKO (*taking offense*). When there's nothing to eat, it doesn't matter if the earth is round or square. Stop pestering me, will you please.

ARKADINA (*annoyed*). Stop it, gentlemen. (Cens.)

page 102 / *After*: It's so uninteresting! — (*Recites.*) Humans, lions, eagles and partridges, antlered deer, geese, spiders, silent fishes that inhabit the waters, starfish, and those beings invisible to the naked eye,— in short, all living things, all living things, all living things, having completed the doleful cycle, are now extinct . . . Already thousands of centuries have passed since the earth bore any living creature, and this pale moon to no avail doth light her lamp. No more does the meadow awake to the cries of cranes, and the mayflies are no longer to be heard in the linden groves. (Cens.)

page 103 / *After*: stop smoking. —

DORN. You should have done it long ago. Tobacco and wine are so disgusting! (Cens.)

page 104 / *Replace*: You've lived in your lifetime, but what about me? I worked in the Department of Justice for twenty-eight years, but I still haven't lived.

---

gressive Russians in the 1870s, but by the end of the century their ideas were considered outmoded.

with: You've lived your life, your room is full of embroidered pillows, slippers and all that, like some kind of museum, but I still haven't lived. (Cens.)

page 104 / *Replace*: So there and all the rest.
with: Everyone's right according to his own lights, everyone goes wherever his inclinations lead him. (Cens.)

page 104 / *Before*: A man should take life seriously, — It's precisely because everyone is right according to his own lights, that everyone suffers. (Cens.)

page 104 / *After*: ridiculous. — It's time to think about eternity.
> *TREPLYOV walks past the house without a hat, a*
> *gun in one hand, and a dead gull in the other.*
ARKADINA (*to her son*). Kostya, come join us!
> *TREPLYOV glances at them and exits.*
DORN (*singing quietly*). "Tell her of love, flowers of mine . . ."
NINA. You're off-key, doctor.
DORN. It doesn't matter. (*To Sorin.*) As I was saying, Your Excellency. It's time to think about eternity. (*Pause.*) (Cens.)

page 105 / *Replace*: **DORN** (*sings*). "Tell her of love, flowers of mine . . ."
with: **DORN.** Well, say what you like, I cannot do without nature.
ARKADINA. What about books? In poetic images nature is more moving and refined than as is. (Cens.)

page 105 / *Replace*: Carriage horses?
with: A carriage horse? Did you say: a carriage horse? Go out there

and see for yourself: the roan is lame, Cossack Lass is bloated with water . . . (Cens.)

page 105 / *After*: This is incredible! —

POLINA ANDREEVNA (*to her husband*). Stop it, I implore you.

ARKADINA. Horse-collars or rye are nothing to do with me . . . I am going and that's that.

SHAMRAEV. Irina Nikolaevna, have a heart, on what? (Cens.)

page 106 / *After*: What can I do? —

SORIN. He's going. He's leaving the farmwork at the busiest time and so on. I won't let him do it! I'll force him to stay!

DORN. Pyotr Nikolaevich, have at least a penny's worth of character! (Cens.)

page 107 / *Replace*: He even sent the carriage horses . . . his crudeness.

with: You know, he even sent the carriage horses into the fields. He does what he likes. His third year here he told the old man to mortgage the estate . . . What for? What was the need? He bought pedigreed turkeys and suckling pigs and they all died on his hands. He set up expensive beehives and in winter all the bees froze to death. The entire income from the estate he wastes on building, and on top of that takes the old man's pension away and sends Irina Nikolaevna six hundred rubles a year out of the old man's money, as if it were part of the income, and she's delighted, because she's stingy.

DORN (*distractedly*). Yes. (*Pause.*) (Cens.)

page 107 / *Replace*: stop lying . . . (*Pause*.)

with: stop lying . . . Twenty years I've been your wife, your friend . . . Take me into your home.

page 108 / *Replace*: Forgive me, I'm getting on your nerves . . . **DORN** (*to Nina, who walks by*)

with: **DORN** (*sings quietly*). "At the hour of parting, at the hour of farewell . . ."

> NINA *appears near the house; she picks flowers.*

POLINA ANDREEVNA (*to Dorn, in an undertone*). You spent all morning again with Irina Nikolaevna!

DORN. I have to be with somebody.

POLINA ANDREEVNA. I'm suffering from jealousy. Forgive me. You're sick and tired of me.

DORN. No, not at all.

POLINA ANDREEVNA. Of course, you're a doctor, there's no way you can avoid women. That's how it is. But you know that this is torture. Be with women, but at least try so that I don't notice it.

DORN. I'll try. (*To Nina.*) (Cens.)

page 109 / *After*: like anybody else . . . — They're modest. Yesterday I asked him for an autograph, and he was naughty and wrote me bad poetry, deliberately bad, so that everyone would laugh . . . (Cens.)

ACT THREE

page 124 / *After*: I can never get any horses . . . — *Enter MEDVEDENKO.* (Cens.)

page 124 / *Replace*: **SORIN**. You're kind, affectionate . . . I respect you . . . Yes . . . (*Staggers*.)

with: **MEDVEDENKO** (*smokes a fat hand-rolled cigarette; addressing no one in particular*). The schoolteacher at Telyatyev bought hay at a very good price. Thirty-five pounds for nine kopeks, delivery included. And just last week I paid eleven. It gets you going in circles. (*Noticing the star on Sorin's chest*.) What's that you've got? Hm . . . I received a medal too, but they should have given me money.

ARKADINA. Semyon Semyonych, be so kind, allow me to talk with my brother. We would like to be left in private.

MEDVEDENKO. Ah, fine! I understand . . . I understand . . . (*Exits*.)

SORIN. He comes here at the crack of dawn. Keeps coming and talking about something. (*Laughs*.) A kind man, but already a bit . . . makes you sick and tired. (*Staggers*.) (Cens.)

ACT FOUR

page 144 / *Replace*: **MEDVEDENKO**. Might I ask, Doctor, which town abroad you liked most?

with: **MEDVEDENKO** (*to Dorn*). Allow me to ask you, Doctor, how much does a ream of writing paper cost abroad?

DORN. I don't know, I never bought any.

MEDVEDENKO. And what town did you like most? (Cens.)

page 150 / *After*: the setting of the action. —

SHAMRAEV (*to Arkadina*). Are they alive?

ARKADINA. I don't know.

SHAMRAEV. She was a highly talented actress, I must remark. Her like is not around nowadays! In *The Murder of Coverley*[5] she was just . . . (*Kisses the tips of his fingers.*) I'd give ten years of my life. (Cens.)

page 150 / *After*: with either of you . . . —

SHAMRAEV (*flaring up, in an undertone*). Well, cut my throat! Hang me! Let him go on foot! (Cens.)

page 150 / *After*: He's nobody special. —

DORN. You get married—you change. What's happened to atoms, substantiality, Flammarion.

Sits at the card table. (Cens.)

page 154 / *After the stage direction*: TREPLYOV *closes the window*. —

SHAMRAEV. The wind's up. The wind's getting up . . . A certain young lady is standing by a window, conversing with an amorous young man, and her mamma says to her: "Come away from the window, Dashenka, or else you'll get the wind up . . ." The wind up! (*Roars with laughter.*)

DORN. Your jokes smell like an old, shabby waistcoat. (Cens.)

---

5 A five-act melodrama adapted from the French by Nikolay Kireev; its climax involves a train speeding across the stage. Chekhov had seen it as a schoolboy in Taganrog and mentions it in several stories of the 1880s.

page 155 / *Replace: then she and DORN wheel out the armchair. Everyone goes out the door left. Only TREPLYOV remains alone on stage at the writing desk.*
with: Everyone goes out left; on stage remain only SORIN *in his chair and* TREPLYOV *at the desk.* (Cens.)

page 156 / *Replace*: Nobody. —
with: It's uncle. He's asleep. (Cens.)

page 156 / *Replace*: (*Looking round.*)
with: And now at him. (*Walks over to Sorin.*) He's asleep. (Cens.)

page 158 / *After*: Time to go. — (*Nodding at Sorin.*) Is he badly?
TREPLYOV. Yes. (*Pause.*) (Cens.)

page 161 / *Replace*: (*Recites.*)
with: (*Sits on the little bench, swathes herself in the bedsheet, which she has taken from the bed.*) (Cens.)

page 161 / *Replace: Embraces Treplyov impulsively*
with: *Tears off the sheet, embraces Treplyov impulsively, then Sorin* (Cens.)

page 161 / *After*: Obstacle course. —
POLINA ANDREEVNA (*following him*). You looked at her the whole time. I beg you, I entreat you by all that's holy, stop torturing me. Don't look at her, don't talk to her for so long.
DORN. All right, I'll try.

POLINA ANDREEVNA (*squeezing his hand to her breast*). I know, my jealousy's foolish, mindless, I'm embarrassed by it myself. You're fed up with me.

DORN. No, not at all. If it's hard for you to keep still, go on talking. (Cens.)